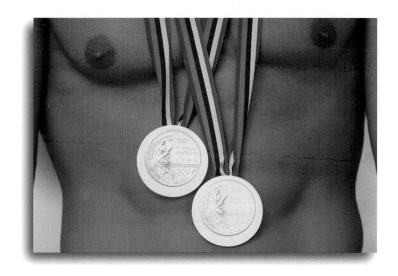

100
Greatest Moments
In Olympic History

100
Greatest Moments

General Publishing Group, Inc.

Los Angeles

In Olympic History

By Bud Greenspan

Publisher, W. Quay Hays
Managing Editor, Colby Allerton
Art Director, Kurt Wahlner
Assistant Art Director, Maritta Tapananainen
Production Director, Nadeen Torio
Color & Pre-Press Director, Gaston Moraga
Copy Editor, Dianne Woo

100 Greatest Moments in Olympic History
is published by
General Publishing Group, Inc.,
2701 Ocean Park Blvd., Ste. 140, CA 90405
310-314-4000

Library of Congress Cataloging-in-Publication Data

Greenspan, Bud.
    100 greatest moments in Olympic history / by Bud Greenspan.
    Special Children's Edition
        p. cm
    Summary: Profiles the accomplishments of one hundred athletes in Olympic competition throughout the twentieth century.
    ISBN 1-881649-67-9
    1. Olympics--History--Juvenile Literature. [1. Olympics--History.] I. Title.
    GV721.5.G65 1995b
    796.48--dc20   95-35678
                                                    CIP
                                                    AC

10 9 8 7 6 5 4 3 2 1

Printed in the USA

Very special thanks to:

Val Ching and Tony Duffy at Allsport, and the Allsport London offices; Pat Olkiewicz and Barry King at the United States Olympic Committee; Wayne Wilson, Karen Goddy and the staff at the Amateur Athletic Foundation of Los Angeles; Bill Bennett and John Dolak at UCLA; Terry Kent at the U.S. Bobsled and Skeleton Federation; Nancy Moore at USA Shooting; Vanessa Osborne, Michael Lira, Brad Slepack, Lindsay Murai and all persons involved in the completion of this project.

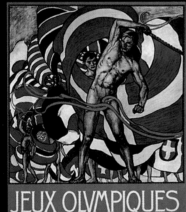

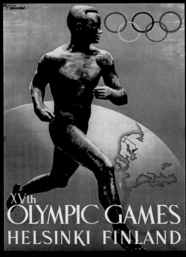

Contents

Introduction

by Juan Antonio Samaranch
President of the International Olympic Committee

It is indeed a pleasure for the IOC President to write the introduction to Bud Greenspan's *100 Greatest Moments in Olympic History*, moments which are cherished by the people of the world.

Mr. Bud Greenspan has chronicled the history of the Olympic Movement for more than four decades, keeping alive the flame of Olympism for thousands of athletes and millions of spectators today and for generations to come.

He has created intimate portrayals of young men and women as athletes, and more importantly as human beings who strive to overcome personal challenges, bringing honor to themselves, their country and most importantly, honor to us all.

Mr. Greenspan has been called the foremost producer, writer and director of Olympic films; more than that, he is an everlasting friend of the Olympic family.

It was in the City of Rome in 1985, after the premiere showing of his film *16 Days of Glory—Los Angeles*, his five-hour Official Film of the 1984 Olympic Games, that I presented to Bud Greenspan the Olympic Order for his outstanding achievements and service to the Olympic Movement.

It is right and proper then, on the eve of the Centennial Games celebration of the modern era, the Games of the XXVI Olympiad in Atlanta, to pay tribute to the man who has captured the heart and the humanity of the Olympics in words and on film and who has now compiled some of these most stirring portraits in this written work, *100 Greatest Moments in Olympic History*.

On behalf of the Olympic Movement, I would like to express our most heartfelt gratitude to Bud Greenspan for writing his *100 Greatest Moments in Olympic History* and his lifelong commitment to the perpetuation of the Olympic spirit.

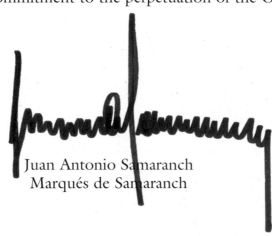

Juan Antonio Samaranch
Marqués de Samaranch

Foreword

by William Porter Payne

President and CEO, The Atlanta Committee for the Olympic Games

Bud Greenspan's vision is unlike that of anyone else on this earth. His eyes function not through his brain but through his heart.

When most of us look at an Olympic athlete, we see a highly tuned physique. Bud's eyes see a human being. We are impressed by finely sculpted muscles; he reveres the discipline and endurance that created those muscles. While we witness the athlete's skills, Bud is taking note of the pride and persistence that developed those skills. And when we watch intense athletic competition, Bud experiences the pure joy of the contest.

It is his uncanny knack for capturing the human drama of sports that has created our vista of shared memories from the Olympic Games. In fact, Bud Greenspan's work and the Olympic Games are synonymous. Now we all can enjoy his vision through his latest work, *100 Greatest Moments in Olympic History.*

Many people have attended every Olympic Summer Games since 1948, as has Bud, but it is Bud's vision that has contributed to our most heartfelt memories. He has spoiled us by intimately sharing what would be otherwise untold, gripping and emotional stories of triumph and tragedy. We learn about Denmark's Lis Hartel, who battles her way out of paralysis in 1952 to be the first woman to win a silver medal in equestrian dressage. And we will never forget John Stephen Akhwari, a marathon runner from Tanzania. His bloody and bandaged form hobbled through the last stretches of the marathon in Mexico City because, he says, his country sent him to finish the race, not just start it.

These stories teach us great lessons in human courage and perseverance. Bud's common thread is the showcasing of the human spirit. Perhaps this is the element that makes his work appealing to everyone, not just those of us who love sports.

Bud Greenspan consistently communicates the humanity of the Olympic Games around the world. His great talent is uncovering those little known stories of individual heroics. How he does this remains a mystery, yet it is a mystery best left unsolved. As his dramas unfold, he touches the highest aspirations of us all through his philosophy that some champions finish last and that winners are not the only heroes. This philosophy goes to the very heart of the Olympic belief that to compete is the highest form of victory.

In the years leading up to the creation of The Atlanta Committee for the Olympic Games and our efforts to host the Centennial Olympic Games, I have watched Bud's films many times. During each viewing, I experience a new emotion, and I see the Olympic Games in a way that is slightly different from before. In fact, Bud's portrayal of the human spirit fueled my desire to be a part of this great endeavor. It is as if Bud Greenspan captured my dreams on film.

Our anticipation of the Centennial Olympic Games grows as we come closer to the moment the Torch is illuminated at Olympic Stadium in Atlanta. These Games will be the greatest experience of my life, and I know my Olympic memories will be enhanced because of Bud's genius.

In the meantime, Bud shares with us through this book his unique vision of historic Olympic Games. You hold in your hands the essence of all that is good and pure about Olympic Games competition. Through Bud's eyes, you will feel the pride and the persistence, grasp the discipline and endurance and, most importantly, experience the joy.

William Porter Payne
President and CEO
The Atlanta Committee for the Olympic Games

Prologue

Selecting any list of greatest moments is at best subjective—particularly those that occurred in sporting events. "Greatest" becomes increasingly difficult when an event such as the Olympic Games is a century old and filled with extraordinary achievements.

Therefore, the word "greatest" could be transposed easily with the word "memorable"—those dramatic, humanistic, inspiring happenings that affected me personally in my life's work—to chronicle the men, women and events who personify the Olympic philosophy—"there are no great people, rather there are great challenges that ordinary people are forced to meet."

In the summer of 1964 Jesse Owens and his wife, Ruth, and my wife, Cappy, and I arrived in West Berlin to film our one hour documentary *Jesse Owens Returns to Berlin*. The idea for making a film on Jesse's life actually began thirteen years earlier in the summer of 1951 after reading an article in the *New York Times*.

The article, datelined Berlin, Germany told of the exploits of the Harlem Globetrotter basketball team, which was performing one of its exhibitions before 80,000 people at the Berlin Olympic Stadium—the scene of the 1936 Olympic Games.

At halftime, as thousands of the spectators left their seats for refreshments, the loudspeaker announcer stopped everyone in their tracks.

"Ladies and gentlemen," the public address system blared throughout the stadium. "Please return to your seats. Now entering through the marathon gate I give you the champion of champions...Jesse Owens!"

Onto the field came 36-year-old Jesse Owens, wearing the same uniform he had worn during his four great gold medal performances fifteen years earlier. Now these many years later he was given the opportunity to take a "victory lap"—the ceremonial run around the track he was not permitted to take in 1936 when the Nazi hierarchy, Hitler, Goering, Goebbels and Hess, looked down upon the field.

Incredibly, the red cinder track was untouched by Allied bombing during World War II. As Jesse smilingly and effortlessly moved around the track a chant began..."JESSE OWENS...JESSE OWENS...JESSE OWENS..." It started as a small rumble and then reverberated through every section of the stadium. The louder the chant became, the more Jesse waved to the crowd.

Soon Jesse completed his run around the 400-meter track and slowly trotted toward a first-row box situated beneath the veranda that fifteen years earlier was the vantage point of Adolf Hitler. This time he was greeted by Ernst Reuter, the mayor of West Berlin. Reuter held up his hand and the crowd quieted. He then picked up the microphone.

"Jesse Owens...fifteen years ago Hitler refused to shake your hand," he said. "I will try to make up for it today by taking both of them."

Mayor Reuter reached out and embraced Jesse and the crowd responded with a mighty roar. Jesse then trotted out of the arena as the crowd continued to cry out, "JESSE OWENS...JESSE OWENS...JESSE OWENS..."

I was chilled after reading the article and knew that someday I would make use of it. So it was in the summer of 1964, thirteen years later, that I found myself with my camera crew in the mammoth empty Berlin Olympic Stadium to start the filming of *Jesse Owens Returns to Berlin*, a one hour television documentary.

It was an eerie feeling standing in the empty stadium where Jesse's victories had upset the Nazi propaganda theory of the master race. Standing there you could all but hear the cries of "Seig Heil" as the audience paid homage to Adolf Hitler. Then, too, one could imagine 80,000 voices singing "Deutschland Uber Alles" that was part of the climax of the opening day ceremonies and played every time a German winner stood on the top step of the victory platform during the Games.

On the second day of filming, I took Jesse over to the starting line of the 100 meters—the scene of his four victories.

I wanted Jesse to be as relaxed and informal as possible, so I didn't prepare him in advance for the questions I would ask.

"Jesse," I said, "what was it like as you were one of six finalists in the 100 meters as the German starter shouted out the command, 'Auf die platze, on your mark...Fertig, set...' just before the sound of the starting gun?"

Without hesitation Jesse replied, "Bud, it was a lifetime of training for just 10 seconds..."

His simple answer became the philosophy of the film and all the future Olympic films I would produce — to pay honor to all those thousands of young men and women who enter the arena, make the attempt and pursue excellence. And because of them, all of us go back to our homes the better for it.

His words would forever remind me that we must pay attention to all those marvelous athletes who give so much of their lives so that we can enjoy the celebration that history will recall as "16 Days of Glory." The Olympic Games is not just the story of those who make it to the victory podium, but those many thousands who fail to gain Olympic immortality by an infinitesimal part of an inch or a fraction of a second.

I have been to every Olympic Games since the 1948 London Games as a broadcaster, journalist and filmmaker. In addition I have gathered rare film dating back to the 1908 London Games, and our library consists of more than two million feet of film.

Through the decades in producing more than 100 Olympic films, I've traveled throughout the world interviewing the great and near great who competed in the earliest of the modern Olympics.

When America's 1,500 meter silver medal winner at the 1912 Stockholm Games, Abel Kiviat, had passed his 91st birthday, we took him back to the scene of his performance. There, more than seven decades later, he was able to recount vividly the Olympic experience of an era long since gone.

We are able to relive the 1936 Berlin Olympics through the eyes of the immortal Jesse Owens, who returned to Berlin with us to recount his four magnificent victories in what history has termed "the Nazi Olympics." And we are able to cheer again the dramatic victory of America's Billy Mills in the Tokyo 1964 10,000 run—one of the great upset wins of modern Olympic history. And we are able to recount the agonizing journey of John Stephen Akhwari of Tanzani—the last man to finish the marathon at the 1968 Mexico City Games, who had the courage and dedication, though severely injured, to finish the race with glory.

So this book is dedicated to the many who through the past century have entered the arena and competed with honor—those who dare valiantly to reach for the heavens—not those alone who were fortunate to grab hold of their star. For it has been written, "The Honor should not alone go to those who have not fallen; rather all Honor to those who fall and rise again."

Acknowledgments

To Sydney Thayer, whose dedicated research made life easier—assisted by Buena Guzman and Baptiste Caraux.

Dan Rarback and Ann Russell for their tireless effort in making our deadline.

Tony Duffy and ALLSPORT for searching their archives for the dramatic photographs.

A special thanks to Wayne Wilson of the Amateur Athletic Foundation, who always had the time for us in researching rare photographs.

To my editor, Colby Allerton, whose suggestions were always "right on."

To art director Kurt Wahlner, for making the book a visual success.

To my friend, George Wallach, who brought us all together.

To Bill Mallon and Erich Kamper, authors of *The Golden Book of the Olympic Games*, for their courtesy in permitting us to reproduce sections from their definitive collection of all-time Olympic records.

And finally, to my old friend Jeffrey Cokin, who keeps us off welfare.

Dedication

To Nancy Beffa—

My partner in life, who makes so many lovely things happen—who showed me that the "impossible" just takes a little longer.

*The most important thing
in the Olympic Games
is not to win but to
take part, just as the most
important thing in life
is not the triumph
but the struggle.
The essential thing is not
to have conquered
but to have fought well.*

—The Olympic Creed

Let the Games Begin...

Jesse Owens

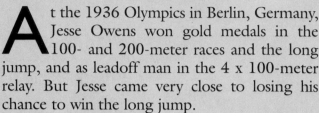

At the 1936 Olympics in Berlin, Germany, Jesse Owens won gold medals in the 100- and 200-meter races and the long jump, and as leadoff man in the 4 x 100-meter relay. But Jesse came very close to losing his chance to win the long jump.

Jesse almost didn't make the qualifying rounds of the long jump, in which he needed to perform well to earn a spot in the finals. In his first two attempts to qualify, he placed his foot over the takeoff board and was charged with fouls. After the two fouls, he had only one more chance. "I was scared stiff that I would blow it on my third and last attempt to qualify," Owens said.

It was the German long-jump champion Luz Long who helped Jesse, even though the two athletes were in competition with one another. "Long came over to me and in broken English said, 'Jesse, let me make a suggestion. I will place my towel a foot in front of the foul line and you can use this for your takeoff. You should then qualify easily.'"

Jesse took Luz Long's advice and used the towel as a takeoff point so that he wouldn't step over the foul line. Jesse then sailed easily through the jump. In the final, he went on to defeat Luz in the long-jump competition.

"It was so gracious of him," Jesse said of Luz Long. "After my victory was secure, Luz was the first one to greet me." The two competitors took a victory walk arm in arm through the Olympic stadium.

"The sad part of the story is I never saw Luz Long again. He was killed in World War II," Jesse recalled solemnly.

In the year before the 1936 Olympics, Jesse had thrilled the world by setting three world records and equaling a fourth in a single afternoon track meet in Ann Arbor, Michigan. And he thrilled the world again at the Berlin Olympics. Jesse Owens's four track-and-field gold medals in the 100 meters, 200 meters, long jump and 4 x 100-meter relay remained unmatched for 48 years until Carl Lewis duplicated his feat at the 1984 Los Angeles Olympics. Add to his victories the fact that he was a black man dominating the Olympics in the racist regime of Nazi Germany, he earned millions of fans (around the world and many in Germany itself!) and became a living legend.

Mary Lou Retton

1984 Los Angeles   United States

At the 1984 Los Angeles Olympics, 36 finalists for the individual all-around women's gymnastic title would compete in four events: uneven bars, balance beam, vault and floor exercise. Sixteen-year-old Mary Lou Retton was considered America's best hope for a medal.

Mary Lou had never taken part in a major international competition before the Los Angeles Games. Ecaterina Szabó, from Romania, was the favorite to win the gold.

Mary Lou scored a perfect 10 in the floor exercise, the third event. With one apparatus left, she trailed the Romanian by 5-hundredths of a point. The situation was clear. If Retton scored a perfect 10 on the vault, the gold medal was hers. A 9.95 would tie Mary Lou with the Romanian and they would share the gold medal. Anything less and the gold medal would go to Szabó.

"You're going to do it...you're going to do it!" chanted Coach Karolyi to his pupil, Mary Lou. "I know you can do it... Now or never. OK?"

Much calmer than her coach, Mary Lou responded with a smiling "OK," and moved to the mat.

Mary Lou eyed the vault, then began her run. She hit the "horse" strongly, with both hands, twirled through the air, then "stuck" her landing. The crowd roared hysterically but Karolyi's screaming could be heard above the noise.

"Ten, ten, ten...ten!" he screamed over and over.

Mary Lou Retton had scored a perfect 10 and was Olympic champion—the first American gymnast to ever win the overall title.

There was one final dramatic moment that is not as well remembered. Each contestant is given two attempts at the vault, and the highest mark is the one recognized. With her victory in hand, Mary Lou didn't have to make a second attempt, but she did anyway. She again received a perfect 10.

Torvill & Dean

1984 Sarajevo   Great Britain

Perhaps if they had not met, Jayne Torvill might be working today in an insurance office and Christopher Dean might still be walking the streets of Nottingham City as a police constable. This was the unlikely background of Great Britain's legendary ice-dancing pair, still considered the greatest team in the history of the sport.

When they finished fifth at the 1980 Lake Placid Games, they couldn't have foreseen that in the future fame would all but eliminate their first names. In the years that followed, the press and public would refer to them simply as Torvill and Dean.

After the Lake Placid Games, Torvill and Dean won three world championships, all high-lighted by ultimate performances of grace, fluency and creativity.

"We don't want to do anything plain if we can put in something interesting," said Christopher Dean. "If something looks plain, it is wrong."

Torvill and Dean were the overwhelming favorites for the 1984 Olympics in Sarajevo, Yugoslavia. The pair were comfortably in front after the first two sections of competition. Next was the "free dance" session. If they played it safe, the victory was theirs. But Torvill and Dean's inspiration was the age-old Olympic motto, "Citius, Altius, Fortius." Swifter, Higher, Stronger…

Skating to Ravel's "Bolero," Torvill and Dean brought ice dancing to a height beyond the realm of the imagination. When the scores were flashed for artistic impression, all nine judges had awarded the pair a perfect 6—a mark that most believe will never be reached again—and with it the 1984 Olympic ice-dancing gold medal.

Dorando Pietri 1908 London   Italy

The marathon at the 1908 Olympics in London, England, is important to this day for two reasons. First, it was there that the official distance of the marathon race was established. Second, it was perhaps the most remarkable finish in the history of the Olympic Games.

King Edward VII and Queen Alexandra of England wanted the race to start on the green lawns of Windsor Castle as a way to celebrate the birthday of one of their grandnephews. The royal birthday present was the reason the marathon distance was established at 26 miles 385 yards—the actual length from the castle to the finish line in London's White City Stadium.

It was warm and muggy on the day of the race, and many of the best runners dropped out from exhaustion. Dorando Pietri, a 22-year-old candy maker from Italy, emerged in the lead position. America's Johnny Hayes, also 22, was 600 meters behind Pietri as the Italian approached the stadium.

Pietri entered the archway looking as if he was about to collapse. When he turned the wrong way, track officials hurried to point him in the right direction. He ran a few yards only to fall in a heap. Some accounts report that Pietri rose and fell at least five times before crossing the finish line in the arms of an official.

As the Italian flag was raised for Pietri, Johnny Hayes crossed the finish line. Pietri was carried off the field on a stretcher.

American officials protested that Pietri was given assistance when finishing the race. They considered this illegal and believed Pietri should have been disqualified. Olympic officials agreed and declared Johnny Hayes the winner.

Pietri recovered and became an international celebrity. Queen Alexandra awarded him a special gold cup for his courage. His fame spread to the United States, where composer Irving Berlin wrote the song "Dorando, Dorando, Dorando."

Joe Deakin, himself a gold medal winner in a relay at the 1908 London Games, said he witnessed Pietri's performance: "The problem was that people along the roadway were giving him glasses of Chantilly instead of water," said Deakin. "Pietri wasn't exhausted. He was drunk."

It may have been the wine, or it may have been the weather, but Dorando Pietri's downfall cost him the gold medal while making him a very famous man.

Lis Hartel

1952 Helsinki / 1956 Melbourne (and Stockholm)   Denmark

Lis Hartel is one of the most revered athletes in Denmark's history. In winning her Olympic medals in the dressage event, Lis had to overcome such astounding obstacles that it's reasonable to call her efforts heroic.

In dressage, a non-jumping equestrian event, horse and rider go through a series of maneuvers without oral command. The rider guides the mount with hand and leg pressure that is all but invisible to the eye. For 40 years dressage was open only to commissioned military officers. Non-commissioned officers, enlisted men, civilians and women weren't eligible.

The 1952 Games in Helsinki, Finland, opened the event to everyone, but the four female competitors were the main attraction. One of them was 31-year-old Lis Hartel.

At age 23, Hartel had contracted polio during her pregnancy. Her daughter was born healthy, and after rehabilitation, Lis was able to walk haltingly with the aid of crutches. But she wouldn't consider herself completely recovered until she could return to dressage competition.

"Why can't my horse be my legs?" she told those who doubted her.

In 1947, three years after her illness, although still unable to use her legs properly, she entered the Scandinavian Riding Championships and finished second. She continued to compete successfully, and was selected as one of Denmark's dressage competitors for the 1952 Games in Helsinki.

Lis amazed the athletic world by winning the silver medal. The victory ceremony was one of the most emotional moments in all of Olympic history. The winner, Henry St. Cyr of Sweden, stood on the top step of the victory platform. When Lis Hartel's name was announced as the silver medal winner, St. Cyr stepped from the platform and assisted her to the second-place position on the podium. The crowd cheered as she took her place.

Four years later, Lis Hartel again won the dressage silver medal in Stockholm. (The main Games were held in Melbourne but Australian quarantine rules made it necessary to hold the equestrian events in Stockholm, Sweden.) Again, as in Helsinki, Henry St. Cyr, the winner of the gold medal, assisted her to her position on the podium.

Jackie Joyner-Kersee

1988 Seoul/1992 Barcelona   United States

At the 1988 Seoul Olympics in South Korea, 29 women entered the seven-event heptathlon. The winner of the gold would be considered "the finest all-around woman athlete in the world."

The heavy favorite to win was Jackie Joyner-Kersee of the United States. She had won the event nationally and internationally nine times in a row. Even more impressive, Joyner-Kersee achieved her amazing feats while suffering from exercise-induced asthma.

At the 1984 Los Angeles Games, Joyner-Kersee had to settle for the silver medal. After the Games, she had married her coach, Bob Kersee, and together they had worked toward the Seoul Olympics.

In the 100-meter hurdles, the first event of the Seoul heptathlon, Jackie won the race and was four points ahead of her own world-record pace, which she had established at the Olympic trials. In the high jump she strained her knee but retained her overall lead. With her leg heavily taped, she got off her second longest throw ever in the shot put. In the final event of the first day,

the 200-meter dash, Jackie was the fastest of all the competitors, but was more than 100 points off her world mark due to her injury.

The long jump, her favorite, was the first event of the second day. She leaped brilliantly and pulled up to within 11 points of her world record. Jackie lost points in the javelin but easily maintained her overall lead.

The last event was the 800 meters. As she came down the homestretch, Bob Kersee was cheering, "Go Jackie…Go Jackie…Go Jackie…" As she crossed the finish line, he leaped over the fence and embraced her, screaming, "You got the world record, you got the world record!"

Jackie had run her second-fastest 800 meters ever to break her own heptathlon world record by 76 points. After her momentous heptathlon victory, Jackie broke the Olympic record in the long jump and won her second gold medal in Seoul. And four years later in Barcelona, Spain, she won the heptathlon for the second time and won the silver in the long jump, qualifying her again for the title of the greatest all-around woman athlete in the world.

Pablo Morales

1992 Barcelona   United States

In 1992 at the Olympic swim stadium in Barcelona, Spain, eight finalists prepared for the start of the 100-meter butterfly. Among them was 27-year-old Pablo Morales of the United States. Morales had held the world record in the event for more than six years.

In the 1984 Olympics, when he was 19, Morales won two silvers and a gold in swimming events. But many thought he'd had a good chance of winning four gold medals. Unfortunately, four years later at the trials, Morales failed to make the 1988 Olympic team. "At the time I believed I would never get back to competitive swimming again," Pablo said later. "I set my mind on attending Cornell Law School. Around the second year of law school, I started contemplating the idea of coming back. My mom was terribly sick with cancer and after she died I made my decision. I told the people at law school that I was taking a year off and started to train again for Barcelona."

At the trials for the 1992 Barcelona Games,

his father and sister were watching from the stands. "I asked my daughter whether she had brought a picture of Mom," said Pedro Morales. "She took it out of her purse and handed it to me. I held it up during the entire race so that she would be watching Pablo."

After eight years, Morales made the team again. In Barcelona he went on to win the 100-meter butterfly, his first individual gold medal. Poland's Szukala came in second and Anthony Nesty of Surinam, third.

"There was a lot of emotion for me on the victory platform," said Morales. "Hearing the national anthem, my thoughts turned to my mother. We had shared so much together when I was growing up…watching the Olympic Games on television together, with her nodding when I told her one day I would win an Olympic gold medal. And now that my time had finally come…and she couldn't be there in person…nevertheless I felt that she was smiling with approval from above."

1936 Women's Relay

1936 Berlin

Germany/United States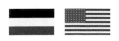

The last day of the track-and-field competition at the 1936 Olympics in Berlin, Germany, promised to be a thrilling conclusion to the event. Some 80,000 spectators, mostly German, were hoping to see a gold medal performance by Germany's magnificent women's 4 x 100-meter relay team.

A few days before, three of the four relay members, Kathy Krauss, Marie Dollinger and Emmy Albus, had finished the 100 meters behind America's Helen Stephens. Only their anchor leg, Ilse Dorffeldt, hadn't competed in the 100-meter dash.

The German women were loaded with speed. They'd broken the world record in their semifinal heat the day before. Their only threat was the American foursome anchored by Helen Stephens. The American team won their semifinal heat in a time that was seven-tenths of a second slower than the new German world record. But in relay racing, seven-tenths is the equivalent of close to 7 meters.

For the final, the Germans' strategy was quite simple. They would build up an overwhelming lead over the first three legs so that even an extraordinary closing effort by Stephens would still leave the Americans far behind.

For three-quarters of the race the German team ran as predicted. Albus, their leadoff runner, gave them a 3-meter lead. Krauss added another 3 meters, and Dollinger gave them an additional 4 meters. As Dorffeldt waited for the final passoff, Germany was 10 meters in front, way too much distance for Stephens to make up.

Then tragedy struck the German team. The first clue to the disaster came when Dorffeldt, as if struck by a bullet, grabbed her head with both hands, her face contorted in anguish. Dorffeldt had dropped the baton. America's Helen Stephens raced to the finish to win the gold medal.

"We were in shock until the next day," Albus remembered more than a half century later.

Stephens, who died in 1994, discounted the German tragedy. Throughout her life she maintained, "I would have won the race even if they hadn't dropped the baton."

The arrow at the bottom right indicates the baton which tragically slipped from the grasps of Germany's Marie Dollinger and Ilse Dorffeldt.

Takeichi Nishi

1932 Los Angeles Japan ●

The charismatic Nishi is second from the right in this photo of the Japanese equestrian team.

The individual equestrian jumping competition, the Prix Des Nations, is a contest where horse and rider travel over a course of obstacles of various heights. The event consists of two rounds, and the winner is the rider with the least "faults." Faults are given for knocking down an obstacle or exceeding the time limit around the course.

At the 1932 Los Angeles Olympics, one of the most popular athletes in the Prix Des Nations competition was Takeichi Nishi of Japan. The army lieutenant, who was born into a royal Japanese family, was the toast of the Hollywood social scene. He became close friends with many legendary motion picture stars of the day. Nishi spoke perfect English and pictures of him at many pre-Olympic parties often appeared in the society section of newspapers.

His popularity was such that the thousands watching the Prix Des Nations cheered for him as much as they did for the Americans in the competition. On his horse Uranus, Nishi completed the two rounds of the course with only eight faults, winning him the gold medal. The admiring crowd gave him an ovation.

Nishi kept in touch with his Hollywood friends after returning home. This close relationship continued until December 7, 1941—the day of Japanese attack on Pearl Harbor.

During the war, Nishi became a colonel, and in a fateful battle, commanded a tank battalion in the battle of Iwo Jima in 1945. After weeks of fighting, his troops were finally cornered inside massive caves with no hope of survival short of surrender. With orders to "fight to the finish," Nishi stayed with his troops and committed suicide with them. He was one of the thousands of soldiers on both sides who lost their lives in what many describe as the bloodiest battle of the Pacific War.

When peace was declared, his motion picture friends said their final farewells. A wreath was sent to the spot where he died. Inscribed on it were the words, "To our dear friend Baron Nishi, with whom we spent so many joyous days."

Milt Campbell

1956 Melbourne

United States

Many consider Milt Campbell America's greatest all-around Olympic athlete, though he's not one of the better known champions. In high school Milt was an all-state fullback and an outstanding hurdler. He was even inducted into the International Swimming Hall of Fame. He competed as a decathlete in two Olympics, finishing second in the 1952 Games when he was 18 years old. He won the event four years later in the 1956 Games in Melbourne, Australia. And during his amazing performance at Melbourne, Milt learned a truly memorable lesson about the spirit of the Olympics.

Campbell started off the decathlon superbly, winning the 100-meter race, and after the first day he was in the lead. The first event on the second day was the 110-meter hurdles. Campbell sped down the course in 14 seconds flat. He extended his overall lead, and with four events left, only a total collapse would deprive him of the gold medal.

In the eighth event, the pole vault, his best leap was almost a foot less than his previous top mark, and he lost valuable points. However, as the 10th

event, the 1,500-meter run, got under way, the gold medal was almost his, but the most dramatic moments of the competition were yet to come.

"As we were going into the last lap, the Russian Kuznyetsov was in front and I was behind him," Campbell remembered. "I was content to stay behind him, but then I heard this voice off my shoulder behind me saying, 'Come on, big boy. It's time to run. You can do better than this.'

"I looked and saw that it was Ian Bruce of Australia, who wasn't even in the top ten. And he kept yelling at me: 'Come on, pick it up…pick it up…stay in there with me…come on, man…you can do it.' So he started to sprint and I started to sprint with him. I couldn't believe it. Here's a guy whom I never met urging me on to win the gold medal. I'll never forget him. Even though Ian had no shot at winning a medal, he was determined to give his finest effort, and he inspired me to reach inside and give my finest as well. They can talk about the true Olympic spirit and laugh at it. But Ian Bruce showed me it does exist."

Oksana Baiul

1994 Lillehammer

Ukraine

The inspiring story of 16-year-old Oksana Baiul of Ukraine reached its climax at the 1994 Olympic women's figure-skating final in Lillehammer, Norway.

Baiul was in second place in an extremely close competition with America's Nancy Kerrigan. However, the day before, Oksana had collided with another skater during a practice session and suffered injuries to her back and leg. The leg injury required three stitches and caused her great pain.

Oksana had endured more than her share of tragedies for such a young girl. Her father left home when she was a small child. Her mother died of cancer when Oksana was 13, soon followed by the death of her grandparents, with whom she then lived. When she was 14, her coach of nine years emigrated to Canada. Oksana was all alone.

Into her life at this time came figure skater Victor Petrenko, the 1992 gold medal winner. Petrenko was coached by his mother-in-law, Galina Zmievskaya.

"My son-in-law Victor Petrenko came to me and asked me if I would take Oksana into my home," recalled Zmievskaya. "He had been giving her money for costumes and food. Victor said to me, 'She is such a small girl, how much can she cost, how much can she eat?' So she became a member of my family and I became her coach."

Baiul's first jump in the free-skating final at Lillehammer was spectacular—a triple lutz, the first of five triple jumps she would perform. Oksana won the gold, scoring a tenth of a point higher than Kerrigan in the deciding artistic category.

Standing on the victory platform, Oksana's thoughts turned to Victor and Galina. The words: "To achieve great things in life, with the help of others, one can overcome the sadness of the past."

There was one more honor for Oksana Baiul. Ukraine is one of the republics which now competes under its own flag since the USSR dissolved into separate countries in 1991. Because of her dazzling artistry, the Ukrainian national anthem was played for the very first time at the Olympic Games.

1956 Yale Crew

America boasted a 36-year winning streak in the eight-oar crew race prior to the 1956 Olympic Games in Melbourne, Australia. The United States was represented by the Yale University championship crew team at Melbourne. On the second day of the Games, this unblemished string of victories was broken. In their qualifying heat, the United States finished third behind Australia and Canada. Only the first two finishers go on to the next round.

To stay in the competition, the United States would have to win the repechage. This race is known as "the race of losers," and features the losing teams from the qualifying heats, and the winner of the repechage is then re-entered into the medal round semifinal. Never in Olympic history had any team won the gold medal after losing its opening race.

Two days later the United States faced Italy, Great Britain and France in the repechage. "We were not taking any chances this time," remembered John Cooke of the American crew. "We won the race very handily. We got some of our confidence back but we couldn't be too cocky. We had beaten a bunch of losers."

Next were the semifinals. "We rowed all out like it was the final," Cooke recalled. "With about three hundred meters left, the Australian coxswain yelled out, 'Ease off, Yanks, you've got it, ease off.'"

For the final, the United States lined up against Australia, Sweden and Canada. Toward the end of the 2,000-meter race, rowing at an incredible 40 strokes to the minute, the United States edged ahead.

The Americans crossed the finish line the winner, followed by Canada, Australia and Sweden. The United States had created Olympic history by being the first team ever to win the gold medal after an opening round defeat.

"I was so tired, my teammates had to help me out of the boat," Cooke said later. "Somehow, they got me to the victory podium. Then I collapsed and they had to cart me off to the hospital."

Bob Beamon

1968 Mexico City

United States 🇺🇸

At the 1968 Mexico City Olympics, Bob Beamon of the United States was in danger of being eliminated from the long-jump competition. In his first two attempts to qualify for the finals, he had fouled by taking off with his foot over the foul line. One more foul and he would be disqualified from the competition.

His friend and teammate, Ralph Boston, came over to him to help. "It was like Jesse Owens and Luz Long all over again," Beamon recalled. "Luz Long came to Jesse's aid at the 1936 Berlin Olympics after Jesse fouled in his first two qualifying attempts. Ralph Boston did the same for me. He told me, 'Bob, you won't foul if you take off a foot behind the foul line. You can't miss.' Basically that's what Luz Long told Jesse, and I took Ralph's advice. I qualified."

Later in the afternoon Beamon created a sensation at the long-jump pit. "I knew I made a great jump," Beamon said. "I heard some of the guys saying things like eight point nine meters…or something. Outside the United States everything is in meters, so I wasn't sure how far I had jumped. I knew it was more than twenty-seven feet, four and three-quarter inches, which was the world record. Then Ralph Boston came over and said, 'Bob, I think it's over twenty-nine feet,' which was almost two feet farther than the world record." Beamon said to Ralph, "What happened to twenty-eight feet?"

After many minutes, the public address system announced the history-making news, and it became official: Bob Beamon's leap, 8.90 meters…29 feet 2 ½ inches.

Bob began jumping up and down, then he was kneeling, holding his hands to his head.

The crowd roared, some questioning whether they had heard correctly. The officials and other competitors were stunned. After Bob Beamon's fantastic jump, for all practical purposes the competition was over in the first round.

Christa Rothenburger-Luding

1988 Calgary/1988 Seoul   GDR

Christa Rothenburger-Luding had a chance to become the first woman to win gold medals in both Winter and Summer Games. At the Seoul, South Korea, Olympics in 1988, if she had won the women's cycling 1,000-meter sprint, she would have done it in the same Olympic year that she won her other gold. Seven months earlier at the Calgary Winter Olympics, she took home the 1,000-meter speed-skating gold medal, to go with the 500-meter gold she had won at the 1984 Sarajevo Games.

Christa married her longtime coach, Ernst Luding, two months after the Calgary Games. He was instrumental in making her a winter–summer athlete.

"We decided that Christa should train in cycling to bridge the gap between the two seasons, winter and summer," said Ernst Luding. "She has the same special qualities for cycling as she does for speed skating—strength and speed."

With 200 meters left in the final 1,000-meter cycling race in Seoul, Erika Salumae of the Soviet Union trailed Rothenburger-Luding. They were playing "cat and mouse." When Salumae made her move, Rothenburger-Luding stayed with her. They were even, wheel to wheel, as the finish line approached. Finally Salumae edged ahead and won the gold medal.

"It was so close," remembers Rothenburger-Luding. "After the final race I talked with my husband, Ernst. We both agreed that the difference was only six inches at the finish."

Christa Rothenburger-Luding stood on the top step of the victory podium at the Winter Games and the second highest step in the Summer Games. And despite not achieving her double gold medal goal, she is still in the history books as the only athlete, male or female, to win a medal at both the Summer and Winter Games in the same year.

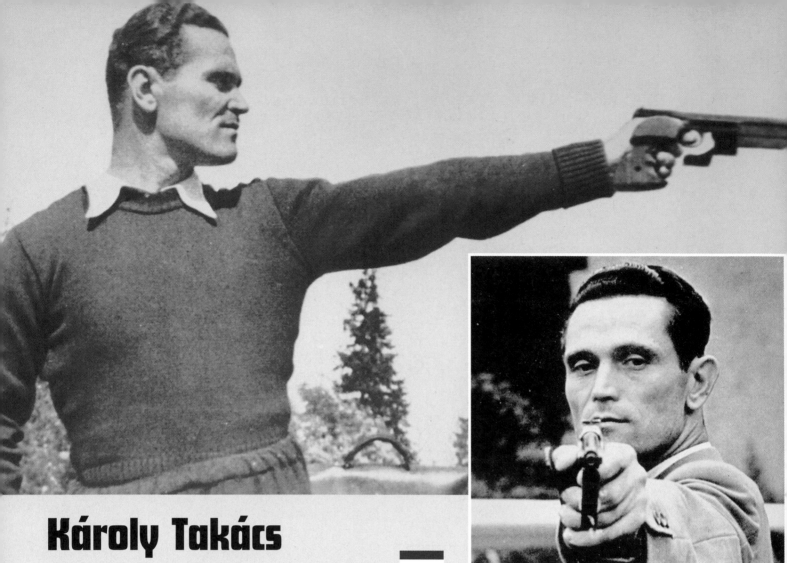

Károly Takács

1948 London/1952 Helsinki   Hungary

In 1938, Sergeant Károly Takács of the Hungarian army was one of the finest rapid-fire pistol shooters in the world. He was a member of the World Championship Hungarian team that was expected to dominate the upcoming 1940 Olympic Games in Tokyo, Japan. But one day on military maneuvers, a terrible accident occurred. A defective hand grenade exploded before Takács could toss it. Tragically, his right hand was blown off.

"As soon as I left the hospital, I made a decision," said Takács. "Why not try the left hand? I practiced all the time by myself, so no one knew what I was doing." In the spring of 1939 Takács surprised his country by winning a pistol-shooting championship in Hungary.

World War II cancelled the 1940 and 1944 Olympics, and it appeared that Takács would never win a gold medal. By the end of the war Takács had risen in rank to captain. All this time he continued practicing.

When the Games were revived in London in 1948, Takács made the Hungarian team. A day before the rapid-fire pistol-shooting championship

he was introduced to the 1947 world champion, Diaz Valiente of Argentina. "Valiente was very surprised to see me," said Takács. "He thought my career was over. He asked me why I was in London. I told him, 'I'm here to learn.'"

Takács won the gold medal, breaking Valiente's world record by 10 points. "Valiente won the silver medal," recalled Takács with a smile. "And on the victory platform he congratulated me. Then he said, 'Captain Takács, you have learned enough.'"

Four years later in Helsinki, Finland, Takács again won the gold medal. Diaz Valiente finished fourth. This time Valiente said to Takács, "You have learned too much. Now it is time for you to retire and teach me."

There were great celebrations when Károly Takács returned to Budapest after the 1952 Olympics. "Everybody was giving me things except for the thing I wanted most," laughed Takács. "So I gave myself a present. No, I gave myself three presents. I had three right hands made especially for skiing, swimming and boxing."

Shun Fujimoto

1976 Montreal   Japan

One of the most prestigious gymnastic titles in the Olympics is the team championship. The Japanese won the team title four times, and at the Montreal Olympics in 1976 they were going after their fifth straight team gold medal.

But during the competition, a severe blow was suffered by one of their star competitors, Shun Fujimoto. He broke his kneecap while performing the floor exercise.

Olympic rules prevented him from using a pain killer. He decided to continue in the competition and try to endure the pain. "I did not want to worry my teammates," Fujimoto recalled. "The competition was so close I didn't want them to lose their concentration with worry about me."

The side horse was his next event. Without letting his coaches or teammates know of his injury, Fujimoto performed the exercise well, receiving a 9.5 out of a possible 10.

His next event would be crucial—"the rings." He'd have to land after a swinging routine that would propel him to the ground with great velocity.

"I knew when I descended from the rings, it would be the most painful moment. I also knew that if my posture was not good when I landed, I would not receive a good score. I must try to forget the pain," recalled Fujimoto.

When Fujimoto landed, he smiled for the judges and held his position for an appropriate amount of time. The judges awarded him a 9.7. Then his leg buckled. By this time the pain was excruciating, for the landing had aggravated his injury further. Fujimoto wanted to continue, but Japanese officials and his teammates would not allow him to stay in the competition.

Knowing they must perform impeccably with only their remaining five members, the Japanese team was inspired to greater heights. They won the title for the fifth consecutive time and dedicated their victory to their fallen teammate, Shun Fujimoto. The margin of victory was 40-hundredths of a point.

Despite a broken kneecap, Shun Fujimoto, second from right, was able to make a significant contribution to his team's gold medal performance.

László Papp

1948 London/1952 Helsinki/1956 Melbourne   Hungary

László Papp of Hungary is perhaps the most unknown "legend" in Olympic boxing. In a sport that has seen Olympic victors such as Floyd Patterson and Muhammad Ali go on to win professional world championship titles, László never made his mark outside the Olympic arena.

At the 1948 London Olympics, Papp fought as a middleweight and easily won the gold medal. "I began boxing during the Second World War in 1944," said Papp. "Before winning my gold medal in London I had fifty-one amateur bouts and lost only one. Forty-seven of my victories were by knockouts! Nevertheless, in London nobody knew who I was until I won the gold medal."

Four years later at the Helsinki, Finland, Olympics, Papp decided to go down in weight and enter the light-middleweight division. Again, he went through the five-bout competition without a defeat, scoring two of his victories by knockouts.

When the 1956 Games in Melbourne, Australia, approached, Papp, now 30, decided to try for his third gold. Just before the Hungarian team was to leave for Melbourne, Soviet troops moved into Budapest to suppress the internal revolution. "The country was in turmoil," Papp said. "Many of the athletes wished to abandon the competition and stay home. We were all saddened because of so much killing and bloodshed. However, I thought I could do best for my country and compete."

In the Melbourne light-middleweight final, Papp faced José Torres of the United States, who nine years later would become light-heavyweight champion of the world. In a close fight filled with flurries of fierce punches, Papp was awarded his third gold medal.

Papp was the first boxer ever to win three gold medals. One year after the Melbourne Games 31-year-old László Papp scored another first. He became the first athlete from a Communist country to receive permission to turn professional. Papp fought 30 professional fights without a defeat. He was as gifted as any boxer, powerful and agile enough to switch weight classes and dominate in the Olympics, but never boxed for a world championship. At the age of 38 he retired and began training young Hungarian boxers for future Olympic Games.

Fanny Blankers-Koen

1948 London

The Netherlands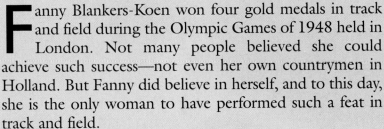

Fanny Blankers-Koen won four gold medals in track and field during the Olympic Games of 1948 held in London. Not many people believed she could achieve such success—not even her own countrymen in Holland. But Fanny did believe in herself, and to this day, she is the only woman to have performed such a feat in track and field.

Fanny had entered the 1936 Olympics in Berlin, Germany, 12 years before the Games in London, and her performance was not outstanding. Many thought that she didn't have what it took to win a gold medal.

But she continued to train, even though she was the mother of two young children. When it was time to compete in the London Olympics, she announced she would run in the 100 and 200 meters, the 80-meter hurdles and the 4 x 100-meter relay.

Dutch newspapers didn't support her decision. "Why is a thirty-year-old mother of two running in short pants at the expense of leaving her family?" a journalist wrote. Fanny's reply was simply, "I will show them."

And show them she did. First she won a gold in the 100-meter race and then in the 80-meter hurdles.

"Even though I had won the two gold medals," she recalls, "I was very depressed. The press would not stop questioning me, and I got even sadder after talking to my children in Amsterdam, who said they missed me. So I told my husband I would not compete anymore and would go home." She had decided not to run in the other two events.

But her husband, Jan Blankers, who was also her coach, saw that she was crying after she reached her decision. "If you stay and compete and win the 200 meters and the relay, you will do what no other woman has ever done in the track and field—win four gold medals. And also remember that only Jesse Owens has done this before." He said this because he knew that track star Jesse Owens was his wife's idol.

"Okay, I'll stay. I'll call the children and tell them they must wait," Fanny said.

She then went on to win two more gold medals.

Fanny returned to Amsterdam and was welcomed like a hero. Holland declared a national holiday to honor her. In a magnificent parade, Fanny, Jan and their two proud children traveled in a horse-drawn carriage through the city before thousands of their adoring countrymen.

Eric Heiden

1980 Lake Placid

United States

In speed skating there is a big difference between the sprinters and long-distance competitors. Sprinters usually compete in the 500 and 1,000 meters, and the distance experts in the 5,000 and 10,000 meters. The fifth event, the 1,500 meters, is considered "no man's land"—too long for the sprinters and too short for the long-distance specialists. At the 1980 Lake Placid Olympics, Eric Heiden of the United States was determined to break the rules and win all five races.

Heiden's first event was the 500 meters. His extravagant quest appeared over after 100 meters, as his opponent led by five-hundredths of a second. But Heiden won in a thrilling finish, inches ahead.

The next day in the 5,000 meters, after one-third of his race, Heiden was almost five seconds behind the competition. But as in the 500, he finished strong for his second gold medal.

Heiden's third race was the 1,000 meters. He won by more than a second and a half—an incredible distance in a world-class sprint race. Two days later Heiden continued his remarkable streak by winning the 1,500 meters by more than 1.3 seconds.

The night before his final race, rather than rest, Heiden was one of the screaming spectators urging on the United States hockey team when they upset the heavily favored Soviet Union team.

The next morning Heiden demolished the opposition in the 10,000 meters, breaking the world record by more than six seconds. Eric Heiden had performed a feat unprecedented in the annals of speed skating—five gold medals in five events.

Joseph Guillemot

1920 Antwerp

France

At the 1920 Olympic Games in Antwerp, Belgium, it seemed a miracle that 20-year-old Joseph Guillemot would run with 15 other men in the 5,000- and 10,000-meter race. Though he was a great athlete, the Frenchman's main claim to fame was that he was still alive.

More than two years earlier, when he was in combat against the Germans in World War I, Guillemot had been a victim of a poison gas attack that left his lungs severely burned. Doctors decided they would try a revolutionary regimen for Guillemot—a training program of easy jogging and long-distance running. They hoped that deep breathing and exercise would help heal his lungs.

No one can explain the complete recovery of Joseph Guillemot. By the time the war was over, the "miracle soldier" was running competitively. He won a 5,000-meter race the year before the 1920 Antwerp Olympics. The scars on his lungs from his poison gas attack during the war were no longer a problem for him. Then the French Athletic Association made a momentous decision…Joseph Guillemot would represent them at the 1920 Antwerp Olympics.

The 5,000-meter race was the long-anticipated debut of 23-year-old Paavo Nurmi of Finland. It was Guillemot's plan to follow Nurmi wherever and whenever he made a move. Knowing that Guillemot was shadowing him, Nurmi began his famous finishing kick for the last lap. But a few seconds later Guillemot began his own finishing kick. Guillemot won by 15 meters!

A few days later the two met again in the 10,000 meters. Though Guillemot passed Nurmi on the last lap to take the lead, the Finnish champion had learned his lesson from the 5,000 meters. Nurmi had kept something in reserve. He sprinted past Guillemot and won by eight yards.

Nurmi is considered one of the greatest distance runners ever, but Guillemot will be remembered as one of the few men to ever defeat the legendary Finnish champion at the Olympic Games. This is even more impressive considering that Joseph Guillemot's nearly fatal war injuries proved to be no match for his determination to rise above them and reach greatness.

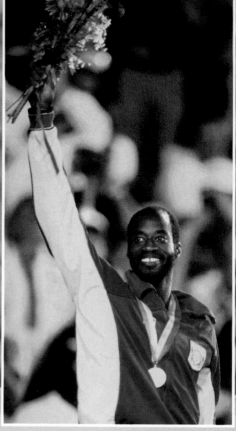

Edwin Moses

1984 Los Angeles   United States

The favorite to win the 400-meter hurdle race at the 1984 Los Angeles Olympics was Edwin Moses of the United States.

At the 1976 Montreal Games eight years earlier, Moses had won the gold medal by one of the greatest margins in the history of the event, defeating his teammate Michael Shine by more than a full second—about 15 meters.

One year after the Montreal Games Moses was defeated by Harald Schmid of West Germany. Over the next seven years leading to the Los Angeles final, Moses remained undefeated in an incredible total of 102 races, including heats and finals.

For Edwin Moses, the years prior to the 1984 Los Angeles final had been filled with turmoil. He was not able to compete in the 1980 Moscow Games because of the American boycott. And in 1982 injuries kept him out of competition.

Several months before the Los Angeles Olympics Edwin's father, who had seen him win at the 1976 Games, died after a short illness.

Sitting in a front-row seat at the Los Angeles Coliseum was Moses' wife, Myrella. "There were so many things on his mind," said Myrella. "His unbeaten streak was still on the line, and before the race he told his mother and me that he was dedicating this race to his dad. And I was so helpless, because I couldn't do anything to help."

Moses' main opposition came from his teammate Danny Harris and Harald Schmid, the last man to defeat him seven years earlier. After 50 meters Moses took the lead.

"The hurdles approach you every three and a half to four seconds," said Moses. "I could feel I was moving away from the others. Things happen so quickly, there is not much time for thinking."

A determined Moses came off the final turn well in the lead and powered over the last hurdle to take the gold. Smiling, he began his triumphant victory lap. Then he spotted his wife and mother, who had left their seats to join him on the field.

Edwin embraced them both and then began to cry. "I won this one for Dad...I won this one for Dad," he said through his tears.

Mary Peters

1972 Munich

Mary Peters of Great Britain still smiles today when people refer to her as an "overnight success." "If that's what they want to call seventeen years of competition, it's all right with me," said the pentathlete. Her Olympic career is a lesson in perseverance.

Mary Peters finished fourth in the five-event pentathlon at the 1964 Games in Tokyo, Japan. In her second Olympics in Mexico City in 1968, Peters captained the women's team, but her career appeared over when she finished ninth.

"When the 1972 Munich Games approached I knew this would be my last chance at winning a medal," said Peters. "I was thirty-three years old and time was running out."

Peters finished second in the 100-meter hurdles. In the shot put, the second event, Mary got off a tremendous toss to win. Peters was again superb in the high jump, winning the event and increasing her leading margin.

"I knew that I had to make the most of my first three events," recalled Peters, "because the long jump and two hundred meters on the second day were not my best events."

On day two, Heide Rosendahl of West Germany, the world-record holder in the long jump, leaped almost three feet farther than Peters. Peters still led, but Burglinde Pollack of East Germany, the pentathlon world-record holder, and Rosendahl both were now within striking distance. If Mary could just stay close to them in the 200 meters, she would earn enough points to win the gold medal.

As expected Rosendahl and Pollack finished ahead of Peters. There was a dramatic delay as the finishing times were converted into points. Finally the scoreboard flashed the news. Peters had won the gold medal, finishing 10 points in front of Rosendahl and 33 points ahead of Pollack!

In her third Olympics and after 17 years of competition, "the old woman" finally reached the top step of the victory podium and became "an overnight success."

Paavo Nurmi

1920 Antwerp / 1924 Paris / 1928 Amsterdam
Finland

At the Olympic stadium in Helsinki, Finland, there is a bronze statue of runner Paavo Nurmi. It was dedicated in 1925 when 28-year-old Nurmi was still in his prime. It is rare that an athlete is so honored in his lifetime.

Nurmi began his Olympic career at the 1920 Games in Antwerp, Belgium. There he won the gold in the 10,000 meters and the silver in the 5,000 meters. He then added two more gold medals in cross-country events no longer in the Games.

In the 1924 Olympics in Paris, France, Nurmi would attempt a "double" that seemed humanly impossible. First he'd run the 1,500 meters, then a little more than one hour later run the 5,000 meters. Nurmi won the 1,500 and 5,000 meters according to plan. This feat still ranks among the greatest individual track-and-field performances in history.

Nurmi then added three more gold medals, all in races no longer on the Olympic program.

Four years later in the Amsterdam Games in the Netherlands, Nurmi won another gold in the 10,000 meters and two silvers in the 5,000 meters and the 3,000-meter steeplechase. His astounding career resulted in a total of nine gold and three silver medals.

At the 1952 Games in Helsinki, Finland, 55-year-old Paavo Nurmi had the honor of carrying the Olympic flame into the stadium as one of the final torchbearers. Nurmi was given a resounding ovation. But he was a man uncomfortable with fame, and left the arena without acknowledging the affection of the crowd.

On October 2, 1973, Paavo Nurmi died at the age of 76. Finnish president Urho Kekkonen, who was a member of Nurmi's 1924 team, gave the eulogy. "When Nature removes a great man," said President Kekkonen, "people explore the horizons for a successor. But none comes and none will, for his class is extinguished with him."

Birger Ruud

1932 Lake Placid / 1936 Garmisch-Partenkirchen /
1948 St. Moritz

Norway 🇳🇴

Ski-jump champion Birger Ruud of Norway was one of those athletes who was more revered in defeat than in victory.

At the 1932 Winter Olympic Games in Lake Placid, 20-year-old Birger Ruud entered his first Olympic event, the ski-jump competition. Each contestant is given two jumps, which are judged for distance and style. In second place after the first round, Ruud got off a spectacular second

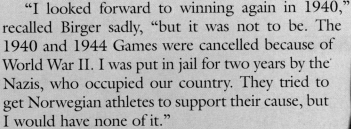

leap. He garnered excellent style points and won the gold medal.

At the 1936 Winter Games in Garmisch–Partenkirchen, Germany, Ruud again entered the ski-jump competition. He hoped to make Olympic history by becoming the first man to win successive ski-jumping gold medals. Ruud was again superb, winning his second gold medal.

"I looked forward to winning again in 1940," recalled Birger sadly, "but it was not to be. The 1940 and 1944 Games were cancelled because of World War II. I was put in jail for two years by the Nazis, who occupied our country. They tried to get Norwegian athletes to support their cause, but I would have none of it."

In 1948 the Winter Games were renewed in St. Moritz, Switzerland. Ruud was 36 years old and an assistant coach on the Norwegian ski-jumping team. The night before the competition, the weather turned ugly, and the Norwegians believed the conditions might be too dangerous for one of their younger jumpers. It was decided that Birger Ruud would replace him. In one of the most surprising comebacks in the Olympic annals, Ruud won the silver medal—12 years after he won his last gold!

All three ski-jumping medals in St. Moritz were won by Norwegians, but the loudest cheers at the victory ceremony were for the man who won the silver—the great Birger Ruud.

Silken Laumann
1992 Barcelona
Canada

Silken Laumann of Canada was the favorite to win the women's single sculls (rowing competition) at the 1992 Olympics in Barcelona, Spain. She had just completed an amazing season. Silken Laumann was the overall winner at the World Cup races and, in a single race in Vienna, was crowned world champion. Honor after honor was bestowed upon her, including being named the Canadian athlete of the year.

In May 1992, a little more than two months before the Barcelona Olympics, Silken was competing in a pre-Olympic race in Germany. Before the race, tragedy struck. "I was just starting to warm up when out of nowhere was this German boat," remembers Laumann. "It crashed right into my right leg, severing all the muscles, tendons and ligaments from midway up my right shin all the way down to my ankle."

Her doctors and coach determined that with rest and rehabilitation, she would get back into competition, but certainly not in time for the Barcelona Olympics, just two months away. However, Silken Laumann had other ideas. After intense rehabilitation and training, she surprised many doubters by being one of the six finalists in the 2,000-meter single sculls at the Games.

Throughout most of the race, Silken Laumann was in fourth place. "With about 1,000 meters to go, I thought I was going to die. I knew I couldn't win but I wanted one of the medals," Laumann remembered. "I said to myself, 'I'm not coming in fourth.' Fourth is the worst position—to just miss a medal."

Once Silken Laumann set her sights on third place, it was full speed ahead, and soon she'd reached her goal.

At the victory ceremony for the three medal winners, one columnist was already writing the lead paragraph to his story: "Canada won four gold medals and one bronze in rowing at the Barcelona Olympics. Let the word go out that on this occasion Silken Laumann's bronze medal shines as brightly in the Barcelona sun as any of the gold."

Despite torn muscles, tendons and ligaments from her shin to her ankle, Canada's Silken Laumann went on to claim the bronze medal in the women's single sculls.

Spiridon Louis

1896 Athens

Greece

For historical and sentimental reasons, Athens, Greece, was the only city that could be considered to host the first revival of the modern Olympic Games in 1896. Greece provided the most athletes, and altogether 245 athletes from 14 countries entered. Thousands of Greek spectators anticipated their country-men would do well in the track-and-field events, in the spirit of the ancient Greek Games.

By the time the competition was almost over, American athletes had won 9 of the 11 track-and-field events, and Australia had won the other 2. The Greek athletes had not won a single event.

The marathon run was scheduled for the final day of the track-and-field competition. Losing this historic race would be the final blow to Greece. Every Greek schoolchild is taught the epic story of the Battle of Marathon in 490 B.C., when 10,000 Greek warriors defeated 20,000 invading Persians on the Plains of Marathon, a seatown some 40 kilometers (about 25 miles) from Athens. After the battle, a lone runner was sent from Marathon to Athens to tell the populace of the great triumph. When he reached the city, he called out, "Nenikikamen," which means "We are Victorious." Then he collapsed and died.

Now, more than 2,000 years later, the marathon would start at the site of the historic battle. The starter's gun sent the 17 con-testants off. At various times throughout the race, runners from France and Australia held the lead. But then an excited horseman entered the stadium at full gallop. The 70,000 people watched for a sign. An excited whisper became a roar. Finally it was confirmed: A Greek runner was in the lead.

The runner was a shepherd named Spiridon Louis. He was exhausted but slowly made his way down the straightaway toward the finish line. The crowd exploded, and the emotional outburst urged the shepherd on.

The Olympic Games had passed its first hurdle, and a Greek shepherd, Spiridon Louis, was mostly responsible for restoring the pride of Greece. As Louis crossed the finish line, many of the specta-tors were whispering those historic words: "Nenikikamen, We are Victorious."

Andrea Mead Lawrence

Oslo 1952
United States

Of all the amazing performances in Olympic alpine skiing, few can compare to the one that took place in the women's slalom event at the 1952 Olympics in Oslo, Norway. It was there that Andrea Mead Lawrence of the United States performed a feat that may never be duplicated.

First Lawrence won the giant slalom by more than two seconds over her nearest competitor. In an event that is usually won by infinitesimal parts of a second, her overwhelming victory had many experts believing the timing watches had malfunctioned.

A few days later Lawrence started down the course in the women's downhill. At the various checkpoints she was far in the lead, but then she fell and was out of contention.

With one event left, the slalom, Lawrence still had a good chance of winning her second gold medal. The event consists of two runs down a course of 38 gates.

On the upper part of the hill, Lawrence skied fastest of all. But in the middle of the course her ski caught a gate, and before she could stop herself, she had gone 10 meters past the gate. Quickly backtracking up the hill to the missed gate, Lawrence continued down the course. When the first run was over, Lawrence was in fourth place, 1.2 seconds behind the first-round leader.

Most experts would have counted her out, since the time she'd have to make up was considerable. But none of the spectators had forgotten her more-than-two-second victory earlier in the giant slalom.

On her second run Lawrence was spectacular, fast and flawless. Her final total time was eight-tenths of a second ahead of the second-place finisher. It was estimated that if she hadn't clipped the gate in her first run, Lawrence would have won the event by at least five seconds.

Andrea Mead Lawrence had done the impossible, and with it became the first American to ever win two alpine skiing gold medals.

Lasse Viren

1972 Munich/1976 Montreal

Finland

One of the great runners in Olympic history was Lasse Viren of Finland. At the 1972 Games in Munich, Germany, Viren wasn't expected to win the gold in the 10,000 meters. With the race less than half over, Viren suddenly tripped and fell, taking another runner down with him. Viren lost more than 50 meters because of his fall. However, with still half the race left, he was able to catch up with the front runners quickly. He took over and amazingly won the gold medal, setting a world record.

A few days later Viren stepped to the starting line for the 5,000 meters against many of the runners he had defeated in the 10,000. Once again Viren was superb. He not only broke the Olympic record but joined his countryman Hannes Kolehmainen, Emil Zátopek of Czechoslovakia and the Soviet Union's Vladimir Kuts as the only men to win both the 5,000 and 10,000 meters in the same Olympics.

Injuries plagued Viren before the 1976 Montreal Games. Several ligaments that had caused him constant pain in his leg had to be removed. He entered the 10,000 and 5,000 meters an unknown factor.

Viren added mystery to his successes by suggesting that he trained on a diet of reindeer milk.

In the 10,000 Viren turned on his famous finishing kick that skyrocketed him to victory. Then Viren held off several challenges in the 5,000 meters to give him his fourth successive gold medal. Lasse Viren had done what no one else had ever done. He won the 5,000- and 10,000-meter events at two successive Olympics.

The day after he won his fourth gold medal the world was amazed to see Lasse Viren at the starting line for the grueling 26-mile, 385-yard marathon. In his first marathon ever, Viren finished fifth.

the Japanese attack on Pearl Harbor in 1941.

"My Asian looks made my life miserable," remembered Sammy. "When I went to public pools to practice, I used to hear people whispering, 'What's that little Jap doing here?' and, 'Does the FBI know if he's a spy?'"

In the 1948 Olympics held in England, Sammy Lee finally got a chance to show his stuff. He did a forward three-and-a-half somersault, a dive he'd invented. "When I hit the water I thought I hit 'flat,'" Sammy recalled. "I was afraid to look at the judges 'cause I thought I would get zeros. Then I saw lots of 'tens' and 'nine and a halfs.' The gold medal was mine."

Lee then retired from sports and continued his medical career. But as the 1952 Olympic Games approached, he had a strong desire to compete again. At 32 Major Lee was up against much younger divers in Helsinki, Finland. But again he was impeccable, becoming the first diver in Olympic history to win two successive platform gold medals.

Sammy contributed to the sport he loved even after he retired from competition by teaching other athletes. His protégé Bob Webster won the platform gold medal at the 1960 Olympics in Italy and four years later in Japan—the only other man to have won successive platform diving gold medals at that time.

Later Sammy became the first coach of a young diver he spotted at a local pool who would one day become one of the greatest divers ever. The boy's name was Greg Louganis, and he went on to win the "double-double"—successive springboard and platform diving gold medals—at the 1984 Los Angeles Games and 1988 Games in Seoul, South Korea.

Sammy Lee

1948 London/1952 Helsinki

United States

Korean-American diver Sammy Lee believed he had a message to send. "Nobody knew anything about Korea," Sammy remembered solemnly, "since we were for so many years controlled by the Japanese. I wanted to show the world what a Korean could do…"

Lieutenant Sammy Lee was unable to compete at the 1940 and 1944 Olympics, which were cancelled during World War II. But the army doctor was determined to make up for much of the frustration that followed him after

Nadia Comaneci

1976 Montreal

Romania

At the 1976 Montreal Olympics female gymnastic superstars would face a formidable opponent—14-year-old Nadia Comaneci of Romania.

In the team competition at Montreal, the Soviet women, as expected, won the title. But it was Nadia Comaneci who captivated the thousands in the arena and the millions of TV viewers throughout the world.

In the uneven bar segment of the team competition Comaneci performed brilliantly, and the crowd was hushed in anticipation as they waited for her score to appear. There was a roar of surprise as the number "1" flashed on the scoreboard. Nadia's many fans soon realized that she had upset modern technology. The scoring system had not been programmed to register a "10," which is a perfect score. The stadium announcer cleared up the confusion: Nadia had indeed been awarded a perfect 10 by judges.

"I knew my routine was flawless," said Nadia afterward. "I had performed it many times before in practice the same way."

Though Romania finished second behind the Soviet Union in the team competition one day later, it was Nadia who again held the attention of the spectators and her fellow gymnasts. In the optional segment, she received her second and third perfect 10s in the uneven bars and the balance beam.

Two days later she was again brilliant in the individual all-around. When it was over Comaneci stood on the top step of the victory podium. She was given 10s again in the uneven bars and the balance beam. The following day, with five 10s already hers, she picked up two more in the individual balance beam and uneven bar competitions.

When the week was over, Nadia's dazzling and precise routines had been awarded seven 10s in winning three gold, one silver and one bronze medal. She also became the first Romanian in history to win an Olympic gymnastic gold medal.

Harrison Dillard

When track star Jesse Owens returned to Cleveland, Ohio, after winning four gold medals at the 1936 Olympic Games, he was given a ticker tape parade. One of the thousands who turned out to greet Jesse was a 13-year-old boy named Harrison Dillard.

"I remember running back home and bursting into the kitchen, yelling, 'Mama, Mama. I just saw Jesse Owens and I'm going to be just like him,'" Dillard said more than a half century later. "My mother just smiled and said, 'Yes, son, I'm sure you will.'"

Dillard had a long wait before he finally got to put his Olympic predictions to the test. The 1944 Games were cancelled because of World War I, so Dillard didn't get to run until the 1948 London Games.

Unfortunately, at the U.S. Olympic trials the man who was predicted to be a certain gold medal winner didn't shine in his specialty, the hurdles. Dillard hit several hurdles and failed to finish the race. However, he did qualify for both the 100 meters and the 4 x 100-meter relay, and won a gold medal in both events at the London Olympics.

Four years later, at age 28, he finally qualified for the Olympics in his favorite event, the 110-meter hurdles. This time, at the 1952 Olympics in Helsinki, Finland, Dillard was determined to win. He was impeccable going over the hurdles and defeated all his opponents. A few days later he ran the second leg on another victorious 4 x 100-meter relay team for his fourth gold medal.

"When I mounted the victory stand for the fourth time," Dillard said, "I was so proud. All I could think of was that time I ran home to my mother after the Jesse Owens victory parade and saying to her, 'I'm going to be just like him.'"

Jean-Claude Killy

1968 Grenoble   France

France's Jean-Claude Killy is one of the greatest all-around alpine skiers in history. But his performance at the 1964 Games in Innsbruck, Austria, was not outstanding, so he had something to prove at his next Olympic meet. At the 1968 Games in Grenoble, France, the downhill was scheduled first.

"Just one month before the Grenoble Olympics, I couldn't win a race," Killy recalls. "The year before I won nine out of ten downhills, but now I was uncertain. I had many doubts whether I could put it all together."

His countryman Guy Perillat was the first skier in the downhill, the most dangerous and thrilling alpine event. Perillat's run was magnificent. He was timed at 1.59.93. It seemed certain that none of the other skiers could match this feat.

However, the 14th skier was Jean-Claude Killy. He beat Perillat by eight-hundredths of a second. Killy and Perillat were the only two skiers to break the two-minute mark, and France won the gold and silver medals.

Killy's next event was the giant slalom which he won by more than two seconds. For the win, he took home his second gold medal.

Finally it was time for the slalom, a two-run event. The day was so foggy that visibility was almost at zero. Killy was in first place after his two runs, but it appeared that Austria's Karl Schranz might beat him. During the middle of his first run, the Austrian suddenly braked. He claimed a mysterious figure had appeared in his path. Schranz protested and was given a second run.

This time Schranz finished without incident. His time was better than Killy's total. For two hours Schranz thought he was the winner, but a review board came to the conclusion that Schranz had missed two gates on his first run and never should have been given a second run. He was disqualified and Killy was named the winner.

With three gold medals, Killy had duplicated the Olympic feat of Austria's Tony Sailer 12 years before in Cortina d'Ampezzo. Killy has gone on to become one of the Winter Olympics' most enduring and popular legends. He is currently a member of the International Olympic Committee and was chairman of the 1992 Albertville Olympic Games in his home country.

49

Greg Louganis

1984 Los Angeles/1988 Seoul   United States

At the 1984 Los Angeles Olympic Games 24-year-old diver Greg Louganis was superb. After winning the springboard event by the most points in Olympic history, he dove in the platform event and again broke a record—by becoming the first diver ever to score more than 700 points.

His final dive was a reverse 3½ somersault in the tuck position. Because this dive has the highest degree of difficulty, it bears the ominous name "the Dive of Death." One year earlier Louganis was competing at the World University Games in Canada and witnessed a Soviet diver attempting the same dive. "I knew something terrible had happened when I felt the tower shake," Louganis said. "I heard screaming and ran to the pool's edge and saw blood in the water. The Soviet diver had hit his head on the platform and was unconscious in the water. One week later he died."

As Louganis prepared for the same dive in Los Angeles, he paused longer than usual. Then he leaped off the tower. He emerged from the water hearing tremendous applause. One judge gave him a perfect 10 and the rest gave him 9s and 9.5s. His final score was more than 10 points better than the magical 700 mark.

Four years later, at the Seoul Olympics, Louganis vied for the "double-double"—successive victories in both the springboard and platform events. In the preliminary round of the springboard, disaster struck. On his ninth dive his head hit the board and he crashed into the water. Fortunately his injury wasn't serious. The next day he won the springboard competition.

Later Louganis found himself in a head-to-head duel in the platform final. Louganis had to be impeccable to win. His last dive was the reverse 3½ somersault in the tuck position... "the Dive of Death."

Without hesitation Louganis walked to the platform edge and dove. The dive was spectacular. Greg Louganis had completed the "double-double" and joined America's women's diving champion Pat McCormick (1952 and 1956) as the only two divers ever to accomplish this feat.

Vera Cáslavská

1968 Mexico City   Czechoslovakia

One of the most moving political demonstrations of the Olympics took place at the 1968 Mexico City Games in the gymnastic competition. The dramatic moment involved gymnast Vera Cáslavská of Czechoslovakia, the undisputed "Queen of the Games."

In Tokyo four years earlier Cáslavská had dethroned the Soviet Union's legendary Larisa Latynina, winning the individual all-around gymnastic title. (Latynina still holds the Olympic record for the most medals won, with a total of 18—9 gold, 5 silver and 4 bronze.)

Cáslavská, at age 26, arrived in Mexico City just two months after Soviet troops had moved into Czechoslovakia to quell free speech. Cáslavská was as spectacular in Mexico City as she was in Tokyo, not only retaining her all-around title but adding a medal in every gymnastic event—four gold and two silver.

But the most poignant moment for Cáslavská took place during the victory ceremony at the conclusion of the floor exercise event. Because they had tied, Vera had to share the gold medal with Larisa Petrik of the Soviet Union. Protocol called for the playing of each winner's national anthem.

A smiling Vera Cáslavská stood tall and straight as the Czech national anthem was played first. Immediately after, the Soviet Union's anthem was played. The smile left Vera's face and she hung her head. There was no mistaking her emotions or the political implications.

One day later there was joy again in the life of Vera Cáslavská. She married Josef Odlozil, who'd competed earlier in the 1,500-meter track race. More than 10,000 fans waited outside the church. When Vera appeared, the crowd's wild cheering confirmed her place as one of the most beloved athletes to appear at the Mexico City Games.

Michael Gross

At the 1984 Los Angeles Games 20-year-old Michael Gross of West Germany would attempt a Herculean task—to swim the 200-meter freestyle, the 100-meter butterfly, and the 4 x 200-meter freestyle relay—all within 26 hours. The 6-foot, 7-inch Gross was nicknamed "The Albatross" because his arms extended in a wing span of more than 7 feet, propelling him through the water faster that any swimmer in the world. When Gross touched the wall at the finish of the 200-meter freestyle, he was more than a body length in front of America's Michael Heath. Gross broke his own world record and became the first West German to ever win a gold medal in swimming.

The next day Gross was back for the 100-meter butterfly. Gross set another world record, his second within 24 hours. One hour and 15 minutes later the 4 x 200-meter freestyle relay was scheduled. Michael Gross was assigned to swim the anchor leg for the West German team.

Gross immediately went after Bruce Hayes, the anchor of the American team, which had a second-and-a-half lead over the West Germans. Halfway through their 200-meter leg, the Albatross drew even. They were both swimming at a pace that would smash the world record. Soon Gross took the lead.

"The dreams I had were coming true," said Hayes. "Before this race I would have terrible dreams that these long arms would be catching me, and now it was happening."

"I was getting tired. It was my third big race," Gross recalled. "I was hoping to go farther ahead and lose contact with him."

In the last 50 meters, Gross' fatigue was beginning to show, and Hayes was inching up to him. Hayes forged ahead and touched the wall first. The Americans broke the world record by more than three seconds. But in defeat the Albatross had swum the fastest 200-meter relay leg ever.

As the swimmers left the pool, a tremendous ovation began for Michael Gross, who with a tremendous effort in both victory and defeat gained Olympic glory.

Billy Mills

1964 Tokyo

United States

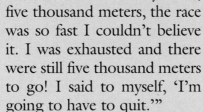

"At a given place on a given day at a given time— something magical can happen." This belief is shared by every athlete during the Parade of Nations at the Opening Ceremonies of the Olympic Games. For one little-known athlete at the 1964 Olympics in Tokyo, Japan, this dream became a reality.

Billy Mills, an American Indian, wasn't the best 10,000-meter runner entered in the Games in Tokyo, and he knew it. Most experts predicted that Mills would do well to finish in the first 10.

"My strategy was simply to go out with the top four runners and stay in contact and hope for the best," recalled Mills. "But when we reached the halfway mark, five thousand meters, the race was so fast I couldn't believe it. I was exhausted and there were still five thousand meters to go! I said to myself, 'I'm going to have to quit.'"

But rather than quit, Mills started to sprint. "I knew where my wife, Patricia, was sitting in the stands.... Together we had made a commitment...and there was really no way that I could quit."

Soon Mills was passing the pack of world-class runners. The crowd was hysterical.

"Something inside me was saying, 'There's still a chance, there's still a chance,'" recalled Mills. "So I started driving. They were fifteen yards in front of me, but it seemed like fifty yards. Then I kept telling myself, 'I can win...I can win...and the next thing I remember I broke the tape.

"A Japanese official came running up to me and he put his hands on my shoulders and with a strange look said, 'Who are you?'" Mills said. "And then I thought, 'Oh my God...I miscounted the laps.' Then he smiled and said, 'You finished...you finished...' and I knew I had won."

Billy Mills had created perhaps the greatest upset in Olympic track-and-field history, and to this day is the only American to ever win the 10,000-meter event at the Olympics.

53

1956 Water Polo

1956 Melbourne   Hungary/USSR

Olympic tradition dating back to ancient Greece calls for fighting between warring nations to stop during the Games. This was to ensure safe passage for the athletes traveling to and from the Games. Sadly, this tradition was violated in modern times. The Games were cancelled during an eight-year period (1912–1920) because of World War I and for a period of 12 years (1936–1948) due to World War II.

Just before the 1956 Olympics took place in Melbourne, Australia, the Soviet Union invaded Hungary, which resulted in much death and destruction. In protest, some countries did not compete, but both Hungary and the Soviet Union sent teams.

The two nations met in the water polo competition. Hungary for years had the best water polo team in the world, and the Soviets were not in their league. The game was a vicious one, with much abuse taking place underwater, out of sight of the judges. Thousands of pro-Hungarian spectators cheered throughout the game as the Hungarians built up a 4 to 0 lead with just a few minutes left to play.

Suddenly a Hungarian player emerged from a melee beneath the water. He had a cut beneath his eye delivered by one of the frustrated Soviet opponents. Hundreds of Hungarians moved from their seats to poolside, ready to attack the team that to them represented the horror that had befallen their country.

Police were called in to hold back the angry spectators, and a conference of officials took place. With much wisdom, the officials decided the game was over and declared Hungary the winner. There was no protest from the Soviets.

The competition continued without further incidents. The Soviet Union went on to win the bronze medal. And the Hungarian team channeled their pent-up anger and national pride into great athletic achievement: They went undefeated in seven matches to win the gold medal.

Olga Korbut 1972 Munich USSR

Probably the most poignant scene at the 1972 Olympics in Munich, Germany, was when 17-year-old Olga Korbut wept bitterly after botching her performance on the uneven bars.

The young Soviet had earlier impressed the gymnastic world with her skill and innovative moves, finishing off her scintillating performances with a captivating smile that endeared her to millions. Television audiences shared in her despair as Korbut's mishaps eliminated her from competing for top honors in the women's all-around.

But Korbut made one of the great Olympic comebacks when she competed in the individual apparatus events. Olga, smiling brilliantly, won two golds and a silver and changed the face of gymnastics forever—and particularly the unemotional image often associated with Soviet athletes.

Olga's personality was not looked upon favorably in the Soviet Union. There her individuality was frowned upon, and she was criticized for becoming a "Western cult star" and exploiting her worldwide fame at the expense of the team.

But in the United States she became an idol and had a great influence on thousands of potential new "Olgas." One United States official said, "Before Olga came on to the scene there were less than 15,000 American female gymnasts. Two years after the Munich Games there were 50,000, and we receive almost a hundred letters a week from young girls wanting to know how they can become another Olga."

Korbut was voted "Woman Athlete of the Year" in 1972 by the Associated Press, but with all the accolades she received, there was one she found the most special.

"In 1973, after the Munich Games, I was brought to the White House to meet President Nixon," she said with her broad smile. "He told me that my performance in Munich did more for reducing the political tension during the Cold War between our two countries than the embassies were able to do in five years."

Teofilo Stevenson

1972 Munich / 1976 Montreal / 1980 Moscow

Cuba

The list of Olympic boxing gold medal winners who went on to become heavyweight champions of the world is a formidable one. It includes Muhammad Ali, Joe Frazier and George Foreman. But the greatest Olympic heavyweight champion chose not to turn professional, though he could have been one of the best. He was the Cuban sensation Teofilo Stevenson.

At the 1972 Olympics in Munich, Germany, the 20-year-old, 6-foot, 3½-inch Stevenson amazed the world with his powerful left jab and sledgehammer right. He won all his bouts up to the final by technical knockout, and then had his hand raised high as Olympic champion without having to throw one punch in the final bout. (His opponent, Ion Alexe of Romania, had injured himself in the semifinal and couldn't compete.)

In the Montreal Games four years later Stevenson continued his knockout string leading to the final. Again he'd have to meet a Romanian, Mircea Simon, for the gold medal. Simon knew of Stevenson's reputation and stayed out of the tall Cuban's reach for more than two rounds. Finally Stevenson hit him with a blockbuster. Simon had enough. Stevenson won his second gold medal.

Incredible financial offers from American promoters were offered to Stevenson. His reply was always the same: "I love my country and they love me. I want to keep it this way."

At the 1980 Moscow Games in the Soviet Union Stevenson, 28, took home his third gold medal. His power was so feared that opponents, rather than having hopes of winning a bout, were happy just to still be standing at the end of three rounds.

Stevenson was now tied with László Papp of Hungary as the only man to win three successive gold medals in boxing. Unfortunately, Stevenson's chance at winning four was dashed when Cuba boycotted the 1984 Los Angeles Games.

Magnar Solberg

Magnar Solberg of Norway is perhaps the least-known champion in the least-known sport on the Olympic Winter program—the biathlon. The biathlon is one of the most demanding winter events—a combination of cross-country skiing and rifle shooting. To win the event a fast skier must also be an accurate marksman.

Solberg was a police officer in Trondheim, Norway. His superior officer, Martin Stokken, a silver medalist in the 1952 cross-country relay, noticed in police training that Solberg was calm in dangerous situations. "Magnar had always been a good cross-country skier and I realized he would be the perfect candidate for the biathlon because there was no danger that bothered him," said Stokken.

As the 1968 Winter Olympics in Grenoble, France, approached, Solberg went through a rigorous training program. Stokken devised a way to simulate the stress of being in actual competition.

"The most critical times during the competition are the few hundred meters before each shooting phase," said Solberg. "Then I had to concentrate on slowing down my pulse rate at least fifty beats in order to steady the rifle."

Stokken's plan for Solberg was torturous. "I placed the target fifty meters away from an anthill," recalled Stokken. "Then Magnar would lie atop the anthill and shoot."

"The ants would crawl up my legs, all over my face, everywhere. It was awful," said Solberg. "I did not believe it at the time but my ability to concentrate under those hot, painful conditions made the actual competition easy for me in the cold."

At the 1968 Grenoble Games, Solberg was the only contestant to have a perfect "no miss" shooting score. This, combined with skiing the course in the second fastest time, earned him the gold medal. Four years later in Sapporo, Japan, using the same training methods, Magnar Solberg successfully defended his Olympic championship.

Dave Moorcroft

1984 Los Angeles

Great Britain

At the 1984 Olympics 14 men lined up at the Los Angeles Coliseum for the final run of the 5,000 meters. Many were predicting that Dave Moorcroft of Great Britain would be the man to beat. In the summer of 1982 he had broken the world record for the 5,000 meters by more than five seconds and was just a half second short of becoming the first to run the distance in under 13 minutes.

Before the Los Angeles Games, Moorcroft had been beset with crippling injuries. He hadn't fully recovered from a stress fracture of the leg, a debilitating attack of hepatitis and a pelvic disorder that on certain days made it impossible to run.

As the 5,000-meter race got under way, it immediately became evident that Moorcroft was in great pain. Sitting in the stands was Moorcroft's wife, Linda, holding their two-year-old son Paul.

"When I saw him warming up I knew something was amiss," Linda Moorcroft recalled. "He was dragging his leg and it was obvious to me that his pelvis had tilted again."

After a few laps Dave Moorcroft was in last place and running with painful, choppy strides. "There was no way I could stay with the pace," Moorcroft said. "I thought of Linda watching in the stands and I knew what she was going through."

As the race moved into its final stages, Said Aouita of Morocco moved into the lead. Moorcroft fought the pain and pushed on. He passed across the finish line a few feet in front of the victorious Aouita to avoid being beaten by a full lap, but had to trudge his way around the track for the final 400 meters. When he finally crossed the finish line he was exhausted and in great pain.

"I had never quit a race before and I was not going to start now at the Olympic Games," Moorcroft explained. "Once you quit, it's easy to do it again. I did not want to set a precedent for the future."

Dave Moorcroft faced his defeat with courage, becoming a greater inspiration for all that is right in the human spirit than if he had won.

Irena Szewinska

1964 Tokyo/1968 Mexico City/1972 Munich/1976 Montreal   Poland

To many Olympic historians there is one track-and-field star who stands above all the rest. Her name is Irena Szewinska of Poland. In her homeland she is still known as "The Queen of the Track."

As an 18-year-old she made her Olympic debut under her maiden name Irena Kirszenstein. At the 1964 Olympics in Tokyo, Japan, she won a gold medal as a member of the Polish 4 x 100-meter relay team and silver medals in the 200 meters and long jump.

A year before the Mexico City Olympics, she married Janusz Szewinska, a sports photographer. At the 1968 Games she won a gold medal in the 200 meters and a bronze in the 100 meters.

Before the 1972 Games in Munich, Germany, she severely injured· her ankle. "The Munich Games were really the beginning of my second Olympic career," said Irena. "After my son Andrej was born in 1970 and then my injury, I couldn't train for about a year."

Nevertheless Irena made it to the 200-meter final and won the bronze medal to continue her Olympic medal streak. After the Munich Games, Irena and Janusz made two momentous decisions. Janusz would become her coach and she would compete in a new event—the 400 meters.

"Through many years of training, Irena had built up a tremendous amount of endurance," said Janusz. "Therefore it was logical that with her natural speed in the sprints combined with her endurance, the four hundred meters would be an ideal distance for her."

Just two years after first attempting the 400 meters, Irena made Olympic history by becoming the first woman ever to run the distance in under 50 seconds! Just this feat alone would have earned her the admiration of many people.

At the 1976 Montreal Games in the 400 meters, Irena finished almost 10 meters in front of the competition. Twelve years after winning her first gold medal, the Polish national anthem was again played for 30-year-old Irena Szewinska. In each of four Olympic Games she had won at least one medal—in all, three gold, two silver and two bronze—to achieve one of the most impressive Olympic careers ever.

Babe Didrikson

1932 Los Angeles   United States

Mildred "Babe" Didrikson of the United States was called the greatest woman athlete of the first half of this century. If it seemed at times that many obstacles stood in her way, Babe always rose above them.

When she competed in the Olympic trials for the 1932 Los Angeles Games, Didrikson won five individual events—the high jump, shot put, javelin, 80-meter hurdles and a now obscure event, the "baseball throw." However, Olympic rules at the time permitted her to compete in only three events. Didrikson chose the javelin, 80-meter hurdles and high jump.

"I could win a medal in five events if they'd let me," Didrikson would say before, during and after the Games.

At the Los Angeles Olympics Babe won the javelin with a great first toss. Next she ran the 80-meter hurdles. Her main opposition was expected to come from her teammate Evelyn Hall. The two ran neck and neck to the finish line. The judges decided that Babe won this incredibly close race by 2 inches! But Hall never accepted the decision. For days afterward she would point to a red mark on her neck, indicating the bruise was caused when she broke the tape.

The high jump was Babe's final event. Both she and her teammate Jean Shiley cleared the world record height of 5 feet, 5 ¾ inches, but the judges intervened with a strange decision. They declared that Babe's style of jumping was illegal, because her head preceded her body and legs over the bar. In those days the standard high-jump technique required the competitor's body to go over the bar before the head. Because of this technical decision, Babe was awarded the silver medal and Shiley the gold.

"The judges were crazy," declared Babe afterward. "That's the way I jumped during the whole competition. If I was illegal on my last jump, I was illegal on my first jump. So if they were right, I should have been disqualified from the beginning."

From her Olympic triumphs Babe went on to become one of the outstanding woman golfers of all time, and in 1950 was voted by the Associated Press as the greatest woman athlete of the first half century.

USA-USSR Hockey 1980

1980 Lake Placid

February 22, 1980, was George Washington's birthday. It was also the day that the United States hockey team would face the heavily favored Soviet Union squad at the Lake Placid Olympic Games.

The Americans were given little chance to win: In six previous Olympic competitions the Soviets had won five gold medals and one bronze. But history was on the Americans' side. The Soviets' only loss came 20 years earlier at the 1960 Squaw Valley Olympics when the United States team won the gold. Being on home ground had been good for the U.S. team then, and hopes were high that this would be true once more, in Lake Placid.

The Americans played their hearts out for two periods, but still trailed the Soviets 3 to 2. United States goaltender Jim Craig kept the team in the game by making one superb save after another.

With less than nine minutes played in the third period, the United States tied the game 3 to 3. Then, at the 10-minute mark, U.S. team captain Mike Eruzione let fly a blistering 30-footer that found the net. The United States now led 4 to 3.

In the final 10 minutes the Soviets attacked furiously, but goalie Craig's inspired performance fought them off. As the last 10 seconds were counted down to the final buzzer, television broadcaster Al Michaels screamed, "Do you believe in miracles?"

The victory was so emotional that many celebrating seemed to have forgotten that the United States still had to defeat Finland to win the gold. The United States met the Finns two days later. As in the Soviet game, the United States trailed after two periods by one goal, 2 to 1. But nothing could stop the Americans in the third period. They scored three goals and won the game 4 to 2. Incredibly, the United States had won its second hockey gold medal 20 years apart—both times in the United States.

Frank Havens

1952 Helsinki

United States

The United States rowing and canoeing team slated to enter the 1924 Olympics was an incredibly powerful group, favored to come home with several gold medals from the Games in Paris, France. And Bill Havens of Arlington, Virginia, was one of the team's greatest prospects. Scheduled to compete in the single and four-man canoeing events in Paris, Bill was favored to stand on the victory podium.

Bill made a decision not to fulfill his Olympic destiny, but in the eyes of some, he still could be considered a hero.

A few months before the American team was to leave for Paris, Havens learned that his wife would be giving birth to their child at approximately the same time as the two-week Olympic competition. Havens had a tough decision to make, for he would be gone a long time—just the journey by ship to Paris took almost two weeks. Havens consulted his wife, family, friends and doctor. All of them assured him that he should go to Paris and be part of the team that was certain to win the gold.

After several days of soul searching, Bill Havens made his decision. He would not go to the Olympics. When his child was born he would be at his wife's bedside. Four days after the Paris Games were over, on August 1, 1924, his son, Frank Havens, was born.

For years afterward Bill was not sure if he'd made the right decision. He'd often dream of standing on the victory platform in Paris. It would take almost three decades before he would realize he'd made the correct decision, for in the summer of 1952 he received a telegram from Helsinki, Finland, the scene of the Olympics. The telegram read:

"Dear Dad, Thanks for waiting around for me to get born in 1924. I'm coming home with the gold medal you should have won." It was signed, "Your loving son, Frank."

Frank Havens had just won the gold medal in the 10,000-meter canoeing event.

Al Oerter

Al Oerter is an undefeated Olympic champion discus thrower, the only athlete to win four consecutive gold medals in the same event in track and field. But it is only by a strange coincidence that Al discovered he had a superior throwing ability.

"I was running the mile in high school," Oerter recalled. "One day an errant discus came skipping in front of me from across the field where the discus throwers were working out. Rather than walk it back across the field, I threw the discus back and it landed about fifty feet behind them. The next thing I knew the coach came running over and said, 'You're finished with the mile; you're now my discus thrower.'"

After easily winning Olympic events in Australia (1956) and Italy (1960), 28-year-old Oerter arrived in Japan for the 1964 Olympic Games. But he wasn't sure he could compete. About a week before the competition, he had torn cartilage in his rib cage in a fall while practicing on a wet field.

"I was bleeding internally. I couldn't move, I couldn't sleep...." Oerter recalled. "The doctors ordered me not to compete. But these are the Olympics and you die before you don't compete in the Olympics."

On the day of the competition the pain was excruciating. Even so, Oerter worked his way to third place. On his fifth attempt, knowing it would be his last attempt due to the pain, Al let the discus fly. Doubled over in pain, he never saw it land. The roar of the crowd forced him to look up. He was stunned to see that his toss had landed almost 2 feet farther than the competition's, good enough for an Olympic record. Al Oerter had won his third gold medal.

Four years later, suffering from a chronic cervical disc injury and wearing a neck brace, Al won his fourth gold medal in Mexico City at the age of 32 and retired. When asked about competing in the 1996 Games, Al replied with a laugh, "I won't try out for Atlanta, but don't count me out for Sydney in the year 2000. I'll be only sixty-four."

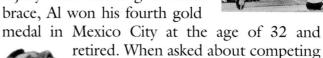

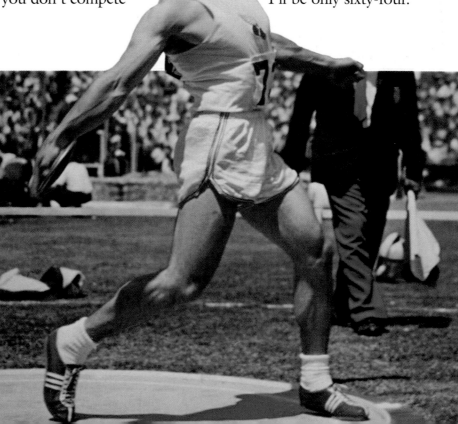

Dawn Fraser

1956 Melbourne/1960 Rome/1964 Tokyo   Australia

Australia's Dawn Fraser was one of a kind both in and out of the swimming pool. Fast talking, cocky and independent, Dawn was constantly at odds with Australian officials for not following the rules. Nevertheless, she was the finest female swimmer of her day and, to many, the greatest ever.

Dawn first gained international fame at the 1956 Olympics in Melbourne, Australia, when she won a gold in the 100-meter freestyle, creating a world record. She followed this by winning a silver medal in the 400 meters.

Four years later at the 1960 Olympics in Rome, Italy, she became the first woman to win consecutive 100-meter freestyle gold medals. In the years leading to the next Olympics she became the first woman to swim the 100-meter distance in under one minute.

Though she was often in battles with officials, she was loved by the Australian people, who value individualism. She made her third Olympic team for the 1964 Games in Tokyo, Japan. When Dawn was selected to carry her country's flag in the Tokyo opening ceremonies, all of Australia rejoiced.

In the 100-meter freestyle duel 27-year-old Fraser would confront the new kid on the block, 15-year-old Sharon Stouder of the United States.

The race was close throughout. Finally Dawn pushed herself and touched the wall first, defeating the young American by 2 feet. Stouder, in defeat, gained glory by joining Fraser as the only other woman to swim the distance in under 60 seconds.

With her victory, Dawn became the only swimmer, male or female, to win the same individual event three times, a record that remains today.

After her triumph, Dawn made headlines when she led a group of teammates to the Emperor's Palace and successfully took home a Japanese flag from atop a flagpole. All of Australia enjoyed hearing of her antics, but Olympic officials were not amused. Dawn was suspended for 10 years, and though the ban lasted only 4 years, at the age of 31, Dawn Fraser's career was over.

Norman Read

1956 Melbourne   New Zealand

When 16-year-old Norman Read of Great Britain was a spectator at the 1948 London Olympics, he became fascinated with the victory of Sweden's John Ljunggren in the 50-kilometer walking race. He decided then that he wanted to become a "walker" and maybe one day compete at the Olympics.

Read began training but soon realized that walking events were not popular in England, so he emigrated to New Zealand in 1954. The Olympic Games in Melbourne, Australia, were only two years away.

He continued his training and wrote to the British Olympic team, asking to be named to the squad. He was turned down. Though depressed by the rejection, Read continued to compete. When he won important races in both Australia and New Zealand, he received an invitation from the New Zealand Olympic officials to join the team. Read jumped at the opportunity and very quickly became a citizen of New Zealand.

At the Melbourne Games Yevgeni Maskinskov of the Soviet Union led throughout most of the race. Read's strategy was to let the Soviet champion set the pace and then take over the lead with about 10 kilometers to go. His plan worked to perfection.

"When I caught up to Maskinskov he had that blank look of surprise and perhaps shock," recalled Read. "At that point I think we both knew that the race was mine."

Read entered the stadium to the cheers of thousands of New Zealanders in the stands. When he crossed the finish line, arms raised high in triumph, he was more than two minutes ahead of the second-place finisher, Maskinskov.

Read took a victory lap, then moved to the infield at the finish line to wait for the third-place finisher. Read greeted the bronze medalist enthusiastically. It was 37-year-old John Ljunggren, whose victory eight years before at the London Olympics was the impetus for Read's journey to the top step of the victory podium.

Gold-medalist John Davis, center, watches teammate J. Bradford (silver) congratulate Argentina's H. Selvetti (bronze) after the heavyweight weightlifting event in the 1952 Games.

John Davis

1948 London/1952 Helsinki

United States

In the long list of American Olympic champions there is perhaps none greater than Brooklyn's John Davis. But whenever Davis is mentioned as an all-time Olympic star, the reply is always the same: "John who?"

John Davis earned the title of "the strongest man in the world" after winning heavyweight weightlifting events at the 1948 and 1952 Olympic Games. But as John explained it, "I was born in the wrong country and at the wrong time." John competed in the pre-television era in a sport that received little attention in his native land. But John was revered in Europe, the Middle East and many other countries.

He won his first world championship in 1938 when he was 17 and looked forward to becoming Olympic champion in the upcoming 1940 Games. But World War II intervened and both the 1940 and

1944 Olympics were cancelled. John was able to win national championships in 1941, 1942 and 1943.

Davis was 27 when the Games were renewed in London in 1948. He easily won the heavyweight gold medal, and the world press greeted his victory with headlines and featured stories. But after returning to the United States, he quickly learned that his victory was not a major event to Americans.

He went to Helsinki, Finland, in 1952 to defend his Olympic title, and won another gold at the age of 31.

Ironically, in 1953 John finally received attention from the American sports press. After 15 years of never being beaten, John was finally defeated by his Olympic teammate Norbert Schemansky.

Once John was listening to a eulogy on the radio for a famous baseball player who had just died. Afterward, he shook his head and smiled. "If you're going to give someone flowers," he said, "make sure they're around to smell them."

John Davis died of cancer in 1984 after a lifetime of athletic excellence. But sadly, on very few occasions was he able to smell the flowers.

Eugenio Monti

1956 Cortina d'Ampezzo/1964 Innsbruck/1968 Grenoble   Italy

Cortina d'Ampezzo, a village 4,000 feet high in the heart of the Italian Dolomite Mountains, was the site of the 1956 Olympic Winter Games. The town's most famous citizen is Eugenio Monti, perhaps the greatest bobsled driver in history.

At the 1956 Winter Olympics Monti won silver medals in both the two-man and four-man events. Because there was no bobsled run at the 1960 Olympics, Monti had to wait another four years for the 1964 Games at Innsbruck, Austria. There he won two bronze medals, but he came away the most admired athlete of the Games.

In the two-man event the British team driven by Tony Nash was in second place after the first run. "When we got back to the top of the hill after our first run," Nash recalled, "we found that our sled had a broken bolt on the rear axle. We were about to quit the competition. At the bottom of the hill

Monti heard of our problem. Without hesitation Monti took the bolt out of his rear axle and sent it up to us. It was an incredible act of sportsmanship and friendship."

The British team went on to win the gold medal and Monti's sled finished third. For his magnificent deed Monti was awarded the De Coubertin Medal for Sportsmanship.

"I do not believe that I did anything that Tony Nash would not have done for me or for anybody else in the competition," Monti says today. "Tony Nash did not win because I gave him a bolt. Tony Nash won because he was the best driver and deserved to win."

At the 1968 Grenoble Games four years later Eugenio Monti reached the pinnacle of his Olympic career. He won both the two-man and four-man events, giving him a career total of two gold, two silver and two bronze medals.

Brian Orser & Brian Boitano

1988 Calgary

Canada/United States

More than 19,000 spectators packed the Saddledome in Calgary, Alberta, to witness the final phase of the 1988 Olympic men's figure-skating championship. The favorites for the gold medal were Brian Orser of Canada, the silver medalist at the 1984 Olympics, and Brian Boitano of the United States, who had finished fifth in the 1984 Games. The press heralded the meeting as "the Battle of the Brians."

"When Brian Boitano was doing his long program I was backstage mentally going through my own performance," Orser remembers. "I could hear his music and I could hear the cheers of the crowd so I knew he had skated well."

Orser knew he must skate the "perfect" program to win. The tension was too much for Orser's mother, sitting in the stands. She left her seat and didn't return until her son's performance was over. She was not alone.

"I did not want to

Brian Boitano and Brian Orser

watch him," said Boitano. "I went backstage and sat in the bathroom and listened to music on my Walkman. I waited five minutes before leaving the bathroom, for I wanted his performance to be over. When I took off my earphones, I heard the last judge gave him a perfect six, so I resigned myself to second place."

The two Brians found out the result in different ways.

"My teammate Christopher Bowman came running over to me with a big smile," remembered Boitano, "and he was nodding his head up and down. Since he was a practical joker, I wasn't sure. Then I said, 'Christopher, if you're playing a joke on me it's the meanest thing you've ever done.' And Christopher said, 'It's no joke…you've won!'"

Remembered Orser, "I looked at the monitor, then at my Canadian broadcaster friends who were giving the results. I saw the bleak look on their faces. Then they shook their heads, 'No,' and I knew that I didn't win."

The victory was given to Boitano by a five-to-four decision—the closest finish in the history of men's figure skating.

Betty Robinson

1928 Amsterdam/1936 Berlin
United States

Betty Robinson was a legitimate first—the first female track gold medal winner in Olympic history. How she got to this point is a remarkable story that reads like pure fiction.

"I was running for the train that took me to school one day," Robinson remembered. "The coach of the track team watched out of the window of the train as I caught up to it and suggested that I should develop my talent. Till then I didn't even know there were women's races."

Five track-and-field events for women were introduced at the 1928 Amsterdam Games in the Netherlands—the 100 meters, 800 meters, 4 x 100-meter relay, discus and high jump.

Three Canadians, two Germans and one American made it to the final of the women's 100 meters. The lone American was 16-year-old Betty Robinson, an unknown high school student from Illinois. In a very close race, Betty Robinson surged past the favorites across the finish line and was declared the winner of the gold.

Next Betty ran the anchor leg on the 4 x 100-meter relay team, which came in second behind the Canadians. In two events Betty Robinson had won a gold and silver medal.

Betty looked forward to competing in the next Olympics. But the year before the 1932 Games tragedy struck. Betty was in an airplane accident and was unconscious for almost two months, suffering severe injuries to her arm, leg and head. She of course missed the 1932 Olympics, but soon began her rehabilitaton.

Incredibly, two years after the accident she was back running competitively. In 1936, Betty was named to run on the United States 4 x 100-meter relay team at the Olympics in Berlin, Germany. Betty was assigned the third leg and would hand the baton to Helen Stephens.

"The Germans were about ten meters ahead when I was about to pass the baton to Helen," said Robinson, "but then I saw the German girl throw her arms to her head and break down crying. She had dropped the baton."

Helen Stephens went on to win, and Betty Robinson had won her second gold medal.

Viktor Saneyev

1968 Mexico City/1972 Munich/1976
Montreal/1980 Moscow   USSR

At the Mexico City Games in 1968 a thrilling competition took place in the triple jump. During this event the previous world record was broken nine times before a winner finally was crowned. That honor went to Viktor Saneyev of the Soviet Union.

"It was an incredible competition," Saneyev later said. "It seems that every time someone jumped, a world record was created. Finally, on my sixth and last attempt, the world record was broken for the ninth time and I won the gold medal."

No one knew then that Saneyev would be a future threat to Al Oerter's record feat (the only athlete to win four successive gold medals in the same event in track and field). Al Oerter of the United States had won his fourth successive gold medal in the discus competition at the Mexico City Games.

In Munich, Germany, for the 1972 Games, Saneyev's first leap was tremendous and earned him his second gold medal.

As the 1976 Games in Montreal approached, a new triple-jump star appeared. He was João Oliveira of Brazil. "I did not know what to expect in Montreal," said Saneyev. "In the triple jump, world records are broken by an infinitesimal part of an inch. Oliveira came into the Games a year after he broke my world record by almost a foot and a half." But Saneyev again came through with a stunning fifth-round leap to win his third gold medal.

Next came the 1980 Moscow Olympics in Saneyev's native land. A victory here would tie Oerter's four-gold-medal record. When Saneyev jumped, many in the crowd cried out his name, believing he had won another gold. But he failed by a little more than 4 inches.

"I knew I fell short, but the crowd was magnificent," said Saneyev. "My teammate Jaak Uudmae jumped brilliantly and deserved to win. For me it was a great honor to end my career with three gold medals and one silver."

Lindy Remigino

1952 Helsinki United States

When the six finalists for the 100 meters lined up at the 1952 Olympics in Helsinki, Finland, 21-year-old Lindy Remigino of the United States had little hope of winning. "I thought I might sneak in for the bronze," he said. Remigino still smiles thinking about it today.

Most experts predicted that the race would be a duel between McDonald Bailey of Great Britain and Herb McKenley of Jamaica.

Remigino had finished second in the United States Olympic trials, but he was up against faster runners from around the world in Helsinki.

The race was the closest in Olympic history, with four men hitting the tape simultaneously. "I went up to Herb and congratulated him because I thought he had won," Remigino recalled. "For about twenty minutes there was no official announcement. But everyone was congratulating Herb and all the talk was that he had won and maybe I was second or third, so close was the finish."

The thousands in the stands were all waiting for the scoreboard to present the results. Finally a Finnish official walked over to Remigino, still standing at the finish line. "Mr. Remigino," said the official, "I think you have won the gold medal..."

"Suddenly the crowd was cheering," said Remigino. "I looked at the scoreboard and it was incredible. My name was first, followed by McKenley. Bailey of Great Britain was third and my teammate Dean Smith, fourth." But all were timed in at 10.4 seconds. The official photo-finish camera showed that Remigino's shoulder had crossed the line first.

A few days later Remigino ran the third leg on the victorious United States 4 x 100-meter relay team—a second gold medal for a man who wasn't even supposed to make the team.

Peter Vidmar

1984 Los Angeles   United States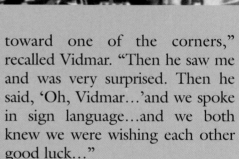

At the 1984 Los Angeles Olympic Games America's Peter Vidmar was locked in battle with Koji Gushiken of Japan for the men's individual all-around gymnastics title. Gushiken was leading by twenty-five-thousandths of a point.

The contestants had to compete in six events—the high bar, vault, rings, pommel horse, parallel bars and floor exercise. Gushiken's last event was the floor exercise, while Vidmar would perform on the parallel bars.

The morning of the finals Vidmar went to the UCLA campus for one last practice session. "I thought I was going to be alone," said Vidmar. "But in the corner was Koji Gushiken. He was reading out loud from what I believed to be a religious book. Finally, Koji stood up and bowed

toward one of the corners," recalled Vidmar. "Then he saw me and was very surprised. Then he said, 'Oh, Vidmar...'and we spoke in sign language...and we both knew we were wishing each other good luck..."

Observing the competition in Los Angeles was Vidmar's wife, Donna. She had the uncanny skill of being able to calculate the scoring with pen and paper, far quicker than the electronic technology that flashed the totals to the spectators.

"Gushiken had just completed his floor exercise and the judges gave him a 9.90," said Donna. "I just wanted to rush down to the floor and tell Peter that he needed a nine point nine five on the parallel bars to win the gold medal. But then I figured Peter knew that."

Vidmar's routine was spectacular, but he took a slight hop upon landing. "I knew that the little hop on the dismount would mean deductions," said Donna. "I expected he would receive a nine point nine, which would give him the silver medal. It was very sad and I started to cry. I looked to Peter and he was still smiling. But I already knew that he had lost the gold medal." She was right.

Vidmar, however, had his moment of glory. He was one of the American gymnasts who won the team title...the first gold medal ever won by an American gymnastics team in 80 years.

t is rare that an athlete is remembered more in defeat than in victory. Such is the case with Italian alpine skier Alberto Tomba.

At the 1988 Olympics in Calgary, Alberta, 21-year-old Tomba won both the slalom and giant slalom events. In Albertville, France, four years later, Tomba made Olympic history when he again won the giant slalom. He became the only alpine skier to win gold medals in the same event in consecutive Olympics. He also won the silver in the slalom.

At the 1994 Games in Lillehammer, Norway, Tomba was not doing as well. He was in 13th place in the giant slalom. He went all out on his second run, but he missed the third gate from the finish and was disqualified.

Four days later Tomba was the first man off in the slalom. After the first run, he was in 12th place, almost two seconds behind the leader.

"I did not think there was a chance for a medal," said Tomba. "There were eleven skiers in front of me with faster first-round times. If there were only three or four I had to beat, maybe there would be a chance. But I must try my best. This might be my last Olympic race."

But Tomba had not given up— and his second run was breathtaking! He was the only man to go the distance in under one minute. The 11 men in front of him couldn't match his superb performance. Only one skier had a chance of beating him—Thomas Stangassinger of Austria, the leader after the first round.

Stangassinger was not able to surpass Tomba's stunning effort and skied the run more than a second and a half slower than Tomba. But Stangassinger's combined total gave him the victory by fifteen-hundredths of a second. Tomba, smiling happily, was the first to greet the Olympic champion.

"It was very exciting to go from twelfth place to second," said Tomba. "And the fact that I won medals at three Olympic Games is something that has never been done in my sport. What more could I ask?"

Afterward one columnist wrote, "Alberto's second run brought back glories of the past. In less than one minute he left a legacy for all those who will follow."

Peter Snell

1960 Rome/1964 Tokyo

New Zealand

Peter Snell is considered by many to be the greatest Olympic middle-distance champion ever. But before the 1960 Olympics in Rome, Italy, very few people outside of New Zealand had ever heard of him.

"I considered myself rather fortunate to be on the team," recalled Snell. "My best time leading to Rome was about twenty-fifth in the world. I thought I would be one of the finalists, but quite frankly the idea of winning the gold medal never entered my mind."

Snell stunned the crowd at the 1960 Rome Games by zooming by the lead runners in the last seconds of the 800-meter final to claim the gold.

After Rome Snell became the world-record holder in both the 800 meters and the mile run, the equivalent of the Olympic 1,500 meters. Next were the 1964 Games in Tokyo, Japan, where Snell would run both the 800 and 1,500 meters.

At the opening ceremonies the 26-year-old Snell was given the honor of carrying the New Zealand flag. A few days later he demolished the 800-meter world-class runners to win his second successive gold medal. Now he would attempt the 1,500 meters. No athlete had won both races since Great Britain's Albert Hill performed that feat almost a half century earlier at the 1920 Antwerp Games.

In the 1,500-meter final Peter Snell and his countryman John Davies were in the lead. "Then it happened," Davies said. "This black 'singlet' [runners uniform], the same as mine, went zooming past me. And there were these great bulky muscles of Snell's legs going down the track away from me and he was actually tearing great big chunks of cinders out of the track...." Snell had completed the 800/1,500 double victory.

Not long ago there was a poll in the *Los Angeles Times* about an 800-meter "dream race" that would include every Olympic and world-record holder of this century. The race would be run by athletes chosen by leading track-and-field experts, both coaches and press. The ballot was secret. All 20 selected Peter Snell as the winner.

Tenley Albright

1956 Cortina d'Ampezzo　United States

Tenley Albright is one of America's greatest as well as most courageous figure-skating champions. When she was 11, she contracted polio. "I was not completely paralyzed, but I did not have use of my legs, back and neck," recalled Albright. "I did get cured and was able to skate, but my parents told me not to be surprised if the other kids wouldn't play with me, fearing they might catch polio."

At the 1952 Olympics in Oslo, Norway, 16-year-old Tenley Albright won the women's figure-skating silver medal.

A few weeks before the 1956 Olympics in Cortina d'Ampezzo, Italy, tragedy struck Tenley during a practice session. "I fell and slashed my right leg with the blade of my left skate," remembered Tenley. "The cut was a jagged one, very bloody, and reached the bone. Fortunately it didn't break any of the bone."

Tenley's father was a doctor, and he immediately flew to Cortina. "Dad patched me up good," she recalled. "But on the day of the competition I was worried. My leg was stiff and my ankle was all taped up."

Tenley had a slight lead over her teammate Carol Heiss after the compulsory figures, which in 1956 represented 60 percent of a skater's total score. As the freestyle event got under way, Tenley would have to test her leg with intricate jumps and spins.

"I was skating to 'The Barcarolle' from *The Tales of Hoffman*," Tenley said. "Suddenly, almost as if orchestrated, the audience began to sing the words, and their voices just thrilled me. I forgot about the injury and just skated. But I must confess the chills were going up and down my spine."

That night Tenley Albright stood on the top step of the podium as the first American woman to win the Olympic figure-skating gold medal.

75

Paavo Yrjola

1928 Amsterdam

Finland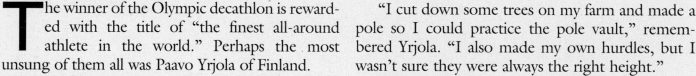

The winner of the Olympic decathlon is rewarded with the title of "the finest all-around athlete in the world." Perhaps the most unsung of them all was Paavo Yrjola of Finland.

Yrjola finished ninth in the decathlon at the 1924 Olympics in Paris, France. After the Games he began a streak of world-record performances that climaxed with a magnificent Olympic victory in the 1928 Games in Amsterdam, the Netherlands.

Paavo Yrjola lived, worked and trained on his family farm about 80 miles outside of Finland's capital, Helsinki.

"I was able to practice in the throwing events with a real javelin, discus and shot put," said Yrjola. "I would throw them as far as I could, and then I would walk to where they landed. I did not have a tape measure, so I only knew the approximate distance."

Yrjola's training in the other events was more complex.

"I cut down some trees on my farm and made a pole so I could practice the pole vault," remembered Yrjola. "I also made my own hurdles, but I wasn't sure they were always the right height."

Yrjola explained how he practiced for the running part of the decathlon: "I calculated that the big rock out there in my field was about two hundred meters from where we are standing. Then I would run to the rock and then run back for the four hundred meters and fifteen hundred meters training. I must have miscalculated my distances, for running in the Olympics seemed a lot shorter than the distance I was running on my farm."

When Yrjola was 73, he said simply, "I was not surprised that I won the decathlon in 1928 and in doing so broke my own world record. Since I trained alone in 1928 nobody knew how well I was doing. But I bought as many newspapers as I could and found out how my opponents were doing. So when I got to Amsterdam I knew what I had to do to win."

Derek Redmond

1992 Barcelona

Great Britain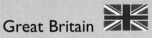

Derek Redmond was a British runner with a chance of winning a medal in the 400 meters at the 1992 Olympics in Barcelona, Spain. At the 1991 Tokyo World Championships, Redmond had gained international fame running with the 4 x 400-meter British relay team that defeated the heavily favored United States foursome.

Unfortunately Redmond's career had been plagued with injuries. At the 1988 Seoul Games he had to withdraw because of a pulled Achilles tendon.

Now, in Barcelona, eight men were lined up to run the first semifinal of the 400. Sitting in the stands watching his son take his mark was Derek's father and most ardent supporter. Jim Redmond described his son that day: "He was in marvelous shape, in good spirits. He was full of confidence and seemed to be the man they would have to beat."

At the start of the race Derek began gaining on the other runners. "I couldn't believe I was going so fast," he said. "I was running so easily it didn't appear to me I was going that fast."

The runner had gone more than 150 meters, moving toward the halfway point. "I was getting ready to make my turn around the bend when suddenly I heard a funny 'pop,'" said Redmond.

He had torn a hamstring in his right leg. The other seven runners finished the race, but now all eyes were on Derek. Though he was in great pain, Derek had decided to carry on, making his way slowly down the track.

Suddenly a man appeared on the track, hurrying to the injured runner. He ran past medics who were carrying a stretcher. It was Jim Redmond, catching up to his son.

"The first thing Dad said as he put his arms around me was, 'Look, you don't have to do this.' And I told him, 'Yes, I do.' And he said, 'Well, if you're going to finish this race, we'll finish it together.'"

It was one of the most memorable scenes of the Olympic Games: a son being helped by his father around the track to the finish line. In defeat, Derek Redmond gained as much glory as if he had won.

Sohn Kee-Chung

1936 Berlin　　　　　　　　　　　　Korea

Sohn Kee-Chung realized one of his greatest dreams by winning the marathon at the 1936 Olympic Games in Berlin, Germany. But it would take him nearly a lifetime to attain a goal that was just as important to him—to run representing the country he considered his home.

Sohn Kee-Chung was born in Korea of Korean parents four years after his country was annexed by Japan. The only way he was allowed to compete in the Berlin Olympics was as a member of the Japanese team, and by using the Japanese version of his name, Kitei Son.

Sohn Kee-Chung was not happy running under the Japanese flag or using his Japanese name. A fervent nationalist, he wanted to make sure the world knew his true feelings. He signed the official Olympic register with his Korean name, Sohn Kee-Chung. To emphasize the point, he drew a small flag of Korea beside his name.

One of the athletes he befriended was the legendary American marathoner John Kelly. "He was very emphatic," Kelly recalled decades later. "He would tell everybody he was not Japanese. That he was Korean. He would keep telling everyone, 'Me Korean…not Japanese….'"

Sohn Kee-Chung entered the stadium as victor after the 26-mile race and was cheered by spectators in the stands who didn't realize the true story of the new marathon champion.

"When they played the Japanese national anthem after my victory, I hung my head," recalled Sohn Kee-Chung more than a half century later.

The climax to Sohn Kee-Chung's marathon victory in 1936 took place 52 years later at the opening day ceremonies of the Olympic Games in Seoul, South Korea, on September 17, 1988. More than 70,000 spectators roared their acclaim and rose in tribute for the runner entering the stadium carrying the flame that would burn throughout the Games—76-year-old Sohn Kee-Chung. After his lifetime journey for Olympic immortality as a Korean, Sohn Kee-Chung had finally reached his destination.

Vladimir Smirnov

1994 Lillehammer

Kazakhstan

For years Vladimir Smirnov of Kazakhstan stood in the shadow of the Norwegian cross-country superstars. But Smirnov's close friendship with Norway's legendary skier Vegard Ulvang and his graciousness in defeat has endeared him to all of Norway. At the 1994 Winter Olympics in Lillehammer, Norway, though he skied for Kazakhstan, a country competing on its own for the first time at the Olympics since the breakup of the Soviet Union into separate countries in 1991, Norwegian fans considered him one of their own.

"There is so much love," Smirnov says of the Norwegian people. "They yell, 'Smirnov... Smirnov... Smirnov,' whether I win or lose."

Smirnov had won two silver medals and one bronze at the Calgary Games. But his most dramatic battles were with Norwegian Bjorn Daehlie. At the 1993 World Championships they raced within inches of each other and crossed the finish line together. At first Smirnov's name was posted as the winner. But 10 minutes later the decision was reversed, and Smirnov was put in second place.

"I was sad for a few days," says Smirnov, "but then something happened that was difficult to believe. I received hundreds of letters from people in Norway, many from small children. Some of the letters from children had paper gold medals attached, saying that I was a fine sportsman and that both of us should have received gold medals."

Because he was getting older, the classic 50-kilometer race at Lillehammer was probably Smirnov's last chance for an Olympic gold. Smirnov had never won a major 50K race, usually tiring badly in the latter stages.

He started off at a blistering pace. At every checkpoint he was the fastest of all the skiers. Smirnov forged on, and when he entered the stadium for the last time, it was evident that finally an Olympic gold medal was his.

At the platform ceremony there were two additional honors for Vladimir Smirnov. The Kazakhstan national anthem was played for the first time at the Olympic Games, and the thousands of flags waving in love and admiration were all Norwegian.

Ducky Drake (far left) coached both C. K. Yang (left) from Taiwan and American Rafer Johnson (right) at UCLA. Though friends off the field, the two were opponents in the 1960 decathlon competition.

Ducky Drake 1960 Rome

United States

During the 1960 Olympics in Rome, Italy, track-and-field coach Elvin "Ducky" Drake witnessed the titanic struggle in the decathlon between Rafer Johnson of the United States and C. K. Yang of Taiwan. Nothing could compare to the 48 hours that confronted Drake during this event. The reason: Ducky Drake was the coach of both men.

While training with Drake at UCLA, Johnson and Yang were like brothers on and off the field. But intense rivalry would take the place of friendship during the decathlon competition.

"They were both my boys," said Drake. "Even though one's an American and one's a Chinese, that couldn't mean anything to me, because I had coached both of them. And I wanted both of them to have the very best chance to win."

At the end of the first five events on the first day, Johnson led Yang by 55 points. What was unbelievable about the competition was the fact that Yang did better than Johnson in four of the five events—the 100 meters, long jump, high

jump and 400-meter run. But Johnson had an overwhelming victory in the shot put.

When they finally fought their way to the 10th and last event—the 1,500-meter run—Johnson led Yang by 67 points. "I watched them sitting side by side on the bench. It was cold and they both had blankets around them," Ducky Drake said. "Here they are, these two close friends, both afraid to turn and look at each other."

To gain the 68 points to win, Yang would have to defeat Johnson by 10 seconds, or approximately 50 meters. This was a distinct possibility, since Yang's best 1,500-meter time ever was almost 18 seconds faster than Johnson's best.

During the 1,500 meters, every time Yang tried to move away, Johnson moved with him. Finally, at the finish line, Yang was only 3 meters in front. It was not enough. Rafer Johnson won the gold medal by 58 points.

"If I had my way, both of them should have won gold medals," Drake said sadly. "They were both my boys."

Ulrike Meyfarth

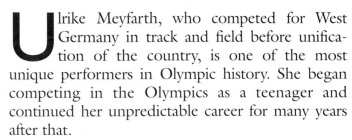

Ulrike Meyfarth, who competed for West Germany in track and field before unification of the country, is one of the most unique performers in Olympic history. She began competing in the Olympics as a teenager and continued her unpredictable career for many years after that.

The inexperienced Ulrike barely made the team for the 1972 Games in Munich, Germany, coming in third in the high-jump trials, which she had to pass before competing in the Olympics. But surprisingly Ulrike won the gold, which made her the youngest winner ever in Olympic track-and-field history. She was 16 years and 123 days old.

Four years later in Montreal, 20-year-old Ulrike Meyfarth failed to make it past the qualifying rounds. Bad fortune continued, as Meyfarth was unable to compete in the 1980 Moscow Games in the USSR because of the boycott, when certain countries decided not to compete in Moscow because of the USSR invasion of Afghanistan.

As the 1984 Los Angeles Games approached, she decided to give it one more try. "So many things happened to me in the twelve years since I won in Munich," Meyfarth recalled. "At twenty eight I was older, more mature and pretty certain I could win one of the medals."

Meyfarth's main opposition was Sara Simeoni of Italy, who had finished sixth at the 1972 Munich Games. Simeoni had won the silver medal in Montreal and the gold in Moscow. Now she would attempt to become the only woman to win the high-jump gold medal twice. This, too, was Meyfarth's goal.

When the bar reached 6 feet, 6¾ inches, Simeoni went over the height on her first attempt. And Meyfarth, without hesitation, quickly equaled that effort. The bar was raised three-quarters of an inch to 6 feet, 7½ inches, 2 inches higher than Simeoni's winning effort in Moscow. The height was too much for Simeoni. Meyfarth sailed over it on her first try.

Ulrike Meyfarth set two more records. She became the oldest female high-jump winner in Olympic history, to go along with the title of youngest track-and-field winner she earned in 1972. Equally prestigious, Meyfarth joined America's discus champion Al Oerter as the only track-and-field athlete to win an individual gold medal 12 years apart in the same event.

Abebe Bikila

1960 Rome/1964 Tokyo   Ethiopia

There is always a first at the Olympic Games, but perhaps the most unlikely first took place in the marathon at the 1960 Olympics in Rome, Italy.

Abebe Bikila of Ethiopia not only became the first East African to win a gold medal, but he was also the first person to run the entire distance of the marathon in his bare feet.

Some sportswriters believed that Bikila's country didn't have the money to supply him with track shoes. The Ethiopian track coach, Negusse Roba, set the record straight.

"Our whole team was supplied with the best running shoes and Abebe was given several new pairs," said Roba. "A few days before the marathon his regular shoes were wearing thin, so a day before the race, he put on a new pair. But they pinched his feet and he complained that they might give him blisters during the race. So he asked if he could run barefoot, for he had practiced many times without shoes."

At the 1964 Games in Tokyo, Japan, Bikila won the gold again, becoming the first man in Olympic history to win two successive Olympic marathons.

Bikila began his third Olympic marathon at the 1968 Mexico City Games but had to retire from the race. He'd suffered a hairline bone fracture in his leg a few weeks earlier but still had wanted to make the attempt.

Tragedy struck in 1969. Driving his car on a dangerous road outside of Addis Ababa, Abebe crashed. His injuries left him paralyzed from the waist down.

A few years later Abebe attended a screening of a documentary film on the history of the marathon. Abebe was an important part of the film. When he arrived at the theater in a wheelchair, he was smiling, and the audience stood as he nodded in appreciation. When he saw himself on the screen, vibrant and in good health as he was in Rome and Tokyo, a single tear ran down the side of Abebe's face and then, unable to control himself, he placed his head in his hands and cried. Abebe passed away in 1973, a national hero and an Olympic legend.

Pat McCormick

1952 Helsinki/1956 Melbourne   United States

At the 1956 Olympics Pat McCormick became the first diver to perform the sport's rarest feat—"the double-double."

In 1949 Pat married her diving coach, Glenn McCormick. Together they prepared for the 1952 Games in Helsinki, Finland.

"The routine never changed," she said. "One hundred dives a day, six days a week, twelve months a year. You've got to remember, too, there was a lot of walking to the top for the platform diving practice. They didn't have elevators in my day."

In the Helsinki Games Pat won the springboard event. Since the springboard was introduced for women at the 1920 Games, American women had never lost. Pat extended the record to seven straight triumphs.

"After I won I remembered the thrill of standing on the top step of the podium," Pat said. "I still get goose pimples when I think of the national anthem. I still get tears in my eyes when I think of it."

Pat then went on to win the platform event.

At the 1956 Games in Melbourne, Australia, Pat won the springboard by the largest margin ever. Now in the platform, she was on the threshold of Olympic history.

"Going into the finals, I was in about third place in the platform," remembered Pat. "Then I said to myself, 'You can't go out now after so many years of hard work without a fight.' So I just sat for a moment and made peace with myself. And that did it. I went up there and performed the two best dives of my life." Pat had won her fourth gold medal.

During her career Pat won 77 national titles to go along with her Olympic medals. In recognition of her completing the "double-double"—successive victories in both the springboard and platform diving events—Pat McCormick won the Sullivan Trophy, awarded annually to the finest amateur athlete of the year, male or female.

Volleyball was introduced as an Olympic sport at the 1964 Games in Tokyo, Japan. A women's team called the Kaizuku Amazons was selected to represent Japan in this inaugural event. The Kaizuku Amazons had an amazing record: They had won 137 consecutive games.

Their coach, Hirofumi Daimatsu, gained as much fame as his team. He designed a training program that many thought was an insult to human dignity. In effect Daimatsu set up a military camp, and the team members were there only to obey his commands. The sessions were brutal mixtures of mental and physical pain. Scrimmages consisted of a nonstop series of dives, rolls and tumbles. Individual sessions were designed to shatter the spirit of each woman. Six days a week the women trained.

"There were many times I wanted to quit," said Masae Kasai, the team captain. "It took me a long time to come to the realization that Mr. Daimatsu's principles were not only important for playing volleyball, but they were important principles for life. In particular, with talent, dedication and hard work, there is nothing one cannot do."

On October 23, 1964, the Amazons beat the Soviet Union team in three straight games—15–11, 15–9, 15–13. On the victory platform all of the team members were in tears. By their side was Hirofumi Daimatsu, without emotion and standing at attention.

"It was a glorious moment," recalled Kasai. "We all cried for two reasons. We had won the gold medal and had fulfilled our own expectations and that of the Japanese people. Even more, we cried because this would be our last game together, and even though we had been through so much pain and anguish it was worth it. I'm sure we would all do it again."

"In Japan I had the reputation of being a devil," said Daimatsu. "However, I believe that when one sets a goal, that one must persevere to achieve such a goal. My goal and the goal of my team was to win an Olympic gold medal."

Keino is getting older, and when he quits, it will be your turn. We want you to be the 'rabbit.' We want you to go out very fast, and neutralize the strength of the other runners.'"

The next day Jipcho burst out of the pack and took the lead. Keino and Ryun were content to stay off Jipcho's punishing pace. But Keino knew exactly when he would go after his teammate. With two laps to go, Keino made his move to overtake Jipcho. Ryun decided to wait. Then, with a lap and a quarter to go, Ryun began to pick up speed. But Keino had built up a tremendous lead and was not slowing down.

"I was passing runners easily, but there were so many in front of me," Ryun said. "With two hundred meters left, I knew that unless Keino faltered, there was very little chance of catching up with him."

The Kenyan strategy worked to perfection. Keino crossed the finish line 10 meters in front of Ryun.

Years later Jipcho was still upset over the Kenyan team strategy, which had successfully manipulated Jim Ryun into starting his finishing kick late and causing him to lose the race.

"It was unfair to people like Jim Ryun," said Jipcho. "Sure, it was good for Kenya. But it was unfair to the other guys."

"I think it does take away some of the credibility of Kip's victory," said Ryun. "In fact, Ben Jipcho came over to me later and apologized for having done what he did. He felt that it wasn't fair. I guess it's a matter of what you personally think. My feeling is that the Olympics are supposed to be man against man—not team against man."

Kip Keino & Jim Ryun

1968 Mexico City
Kenya/United States

The 1,500-meter run at the 1968 Mexico City Olympics promised to be a thrilling duel between the world-record holder, Jim Ryun of the United States, and Kip Keino of Kenya.

In his semifinal, Ryun had defeated Keino. Kenyan officials decided they needed a plan to beat Ryun. They conferred with Ben Jipcho, Keino's teammate.

"The night before the final the Kenyan officials spoke with me," Jipcho recalled. "They said, 'Jipcho, you are still young and have a bright future. Kip

Carl Lewis 1984 Los Angeles

United States

"Jesse Owens was my inspiration," said American Carl Lewis about the 1936 Berlin Olympic champion. Today it is universally known that Carl Lewis duplicated Owens' feat of winning four gold medals in the 100 meters, 200 meters, long jump and as part of the 4 x 100-meter relay team at the 1984 Los Angeles Olympics.

In three Olympic Games Carl Lewis has established himself as an athletic phenomenon. After the Los Angeles Games he came back four years later in Seoul, South Korea, to win two more gold—in the 100 meters and long jump—and a silver in the 200 meters. At the 1992 Olympics in Barcelona, Spain, at age 31, he won his seventh and eighth gold medals with his third straight long-jump victory and then as anchor man on the 4 x 100-meter relay team.

Yet through it all, Lewis has never reached the revered status that his country has reserved for his idol, Jesse Owens. But Carl Lewis is still patriotic. He demonstrated this while taking his victory lap at the Los Angeles Games.

"I felt so much pride for the USA, I just wanted to grab something American," said Lewis. "I was going around the turn after the race and saw this big American flag in the stands. I beckoned for the owner to come down with the flag and I borrowed it from him. His mouth dropped open and he was in shock. So I ran around with the flag and then I returned and handed it back to him..."

How would Carl Lewis want to be remembered?

"Many people have said, 'You can't do that, Carl. It can't be done. A world-class athlete cannot do what you've done...to endure so long.' Well, I feel there are no limitations if you broaden your horizons. If you don't succeed you haven't failed, because you can't fail if you've tried your hardest. So I hope I can just be remembered as someone who has inspired people and led them to do things they never thought they could do."

Billy Fiske

Although everyone called him Billy, his full name was William Mead Lindsley Fiske III. By whatever name, he'll be remembered as America's greatest Olympic and war hero, a man of many firsts.

Billy Fiske's family spent their winters in St. Moritz, Switzerland. There Fiske learned to drive a bobsled and was known as a daredevil. When the 1928 St. Moritz Olympics were only a few months away, Fiske was selected to drive one of the United States sleds entered in the dangerous four-man bobsled event. He was only 16 years old! Fiske drove his team fearlessly to victory and became the youngest man ever to win a gold medal at the Winter Olympics.

Four years later Fiske was given the honor of carrying the American flag in the opening day ceremonies of the Lake Placid Olympic Games. And he easily won his second gold medal driving the four-man sled, the first man ever to pilot a team to two consecutive gold medals in bobsledding.

When World War II began in 1939, Billy became one of several Americans to join Great Britain's Royal Air Force as a volunteer. When the Battle of Britain began, 29-year-old Billy Fiske and his comrades flew numerous missions to defend London from German bombing raids, and he was officially credited with several personal and partial "kills."

On August 16, 1940, Billy again took to the skies. In combat with a German bomber, his engine was hit. His plane caught fire, but even though he was badly burned, Billy was able to land. He was rushed to the hospital and the prognosis for recovery was good. However, the following morning the stunning news was released that Billy had died of shock from his wounds.

Today a memorial plaque to him remains at St. Paul's Cathedral in London. It reads: "To Pilot Officer William Mead Lindsley Fiske III...an American citizen who died that England might live."

In life Billy Fiske was a man of many firsts. So, too, in death. Billy Fiske was the first American pilot to be killed in World War II.

Billy Fiske, shown at right as driver of the USA four man bobsled and in inset in British military uniform, was both an enigma and a man of great courage.

Sonja Henie

1928 St. Moritz/1932 Lake Placid/1936 Garmisch-Partenkirchen

Norway

Perhaps no athlete has had a greater influence on a sport than Sonja Henie, the famous figure skater. Both her Olympic medals and her motion pictures remain as a testament to her talent both in and out of competition.

After winning Norway's national championship, 11-year-old Sonja competed in the first Winter Olympic Games in 1924 in Chamonix, France. She finished last in the competition.

Under the guidance of her father, plans were made for the next Olympics. Wilhelm Henie had grandiose ideas. They would combine Sonja's ballet and athletic ability to create a dramatic program of jumps and spins that at the time was considered revolutionary. Also, Sonja would be costumed in short skirts instead of ankle-length dresses.

The plan worked to perfection. In 1927, when she was 14, she won her first world championship. The following year in St. Moritz, Switzerland, she won her first Olympic gold medal.

Sonja continued to win world championships, and at the 1932 Lake Placid Games easily won her second Olympic gold medal.

"It was impossible to beat her," recalled Vivi-Anne Hulten, the Swede who finished fifth at the 1932 Games. "Her dad spent lots of money on her practice sessions and she was always wearing makeup and beautiful clothes. Most of the competitors resented her because in those days amateurs didn't do that..."

Sonja's world championship victories continued between Lake Placid and the 1936 Olympics in Garmisch-Partenkirchen, Germany. She would win 10 world championships in all.

At the 1936 Games she won her third gold medal. After this she began a career in motion pictures and as a star of ice shows that made her millions for more than a decade. To this day she is the most commercially successful of all the Olympic champions, even though she made her last film almost a half century ago.

George S. Patton

The five-event modern pentathlon was introduced on the Olympic program at the 1912 Games in Stockholm, Sweden. The competition included horseback riding, fencing, pistol shooting, swimming and running.

This challenging competition was based on the skills required of a soldier delivering a message by horseback. If he was confronted by the enemy, he would be forced to dismount and duel with a sword in order to escape. Continuing his mission, he could shoot his way out of danger. Then the messenger might have to swim across a river and run almost 3 miles before he finally delivered the message.

At the 1912 Games Swedish officers won the gold, silver and bronze medals. The only "outsider" who gave them any competition was 26-year-old United States Army Lieutenant George S. Patton, who went on to become one of the most brilliant and controversial generals of World War II, with the nickname "Blood and Guts."

Patton was proficient in all five events. He finished seventh in swimming, fourth in fencing, sixth in riding and third in running. His combined total placed him in a position to win a medal, and quite possibly the gold.

But a major controversy had arisen in Patton's first event—pistol shooting. Patton was renowned for shooting with uncanny precision. But officials claimed that one of his attempts had completely missed the target.

Patton and United States officials argued that this shot had actually passed through the hole of a previous shot, which is why there was no mark on the target. The protest was denied. Patton finished in 21st place in pistol shooting. His combined total in the five events earned him fifth place in the competition.

During World War II General Patton became internationally known for wearing pearl-handled pistols. Romantic history writers have claimed that Patton wore the pistols to remind himself in battle "that nothing is certain."

George S. Patton (right) on his way to fourth place in the fencing event in the pentathlon of the 1912 Games. Some bad luck in the shooting event may have cost Patton the gold medal. In background: The field in Stockholm where the pentathlon was contested.

his second gold medal in world-record time in the 1,500 meters.

Koss had held the world record for the 10,000 meters for more than three years. When the race began, Koss was spectacular, quickly skating to a large lead over Frank Dittrich of Germany. "It was crazy. The ice was so fast," said Koss afterward. "I was getting farther and farther ahead of Frank Dittrich and soon I was passing him. That is impossible to believe. I keep saying to myself, 'Wow, this is something!' I was tired, but the crowd urged me on. It was unbelievable."

When he crossed the finish line Koss looked eagerly to the scoreboard. Then he raised his arms skyward in a victory salute. He had broken his own world record by an amazing 13 seconds!

After his victory Koss announced he would donate his $30,000 prize money to Olympic Aid, a Norwegian charity to assist children in war-torn areas such as Sarajevo, site of the 1984 Winter Olympics.

"I saw all those terrible pictures of the people of Sarajevo, particularly the children. I figured how lucky I have been," said Koss, "and I thought it right that I should share it with those who really need it."

After making his generous donation and in breaking three world records, Johann Koss had become a living example of the words that have sent Olympians into the arena for decades: "Never look to the ground for your next step. Greatness belongs to those who look to the horizon."

Johann Olav Koss

1994 Lillehammer Norway

"Koss Is Boss" was the watchword inscribed on banners at the Viking Ship Arena in Lillehammer, Norway, where the 1994 Olympic speed-skating program took place. The Norwegian crowd sang the familiar "Victory Is Ours" as their compatriot Johann Olav Koss appeared on the ice for the 10,000-meter event. Koss had already proved those words to be true. Earlier in the Games he had won the 5,000 meters, creating a world record. Koss then won

Eddie Eagan

1920 Antwerp/1932 Lake Placid

United States

Eddie Eagan made the United States Olympic boxing team in 1920 and won the light-heavyweight gold medal in Antwerp. Afterward he became an amateur champion in both Great Britain and the United States.

"He was afraid of nothing," said his wife, Peggy. "He was really a world champion. He and a friend took a trip around the world and in every country Eddie challenged the amateur champion and finished the tour undefeated. So when you talk about undefeated champions, my husband was one of them."

With his Olympic days apparently over, Eagan started a successful law practice. His credentials were impeccable—he was a Yale University and Harvard Law School graduate and a Rhodes scholar.

As the 1932 Lake Placid Olympic Winter Games approached, Eagan had a momentous meeting with his friend Jay O'Brien, the chairman of the United States bobsled selection committee. "One night Eddie came back from a dinner with Jay and said, 'Guess what? I'm on the United States bobsled team,' Peggy Eagan recalled. I was shocked because Eddie had never been on a bobsled before."

The driver of the bobsled would be Billy Fiske, a socialite daredevil who four years earlier drove his sled to victory at the 1928 St. Moritz Olympics. Eddie Eagan would be in the number two spot, followed by Clifford Gray, a successful songwriter. The brakeman was Jay O'Brien, the U.S. bobsled committee chairman.

The strangest foursome ever assembled for a bobsled event clinched a victory by more than two seconds.

For Billy Fiske and Clifford Gray, it was their second successive Olympic bobsled victory. For Eddie Eagan it was his second gold medal garnered 12 years after his boxing victory. It was a singular honor for Eddie, one that still remains today. He is the only athlete, male or female, to have won gold medals at both the Winter and Summer Olympics.

Eddie Eagan is the only individual to have won a gold medal in both the Summer and Winter Games: as light heavyweight champion in 1920 (top) and as member of the USA's gold medal-winning, four-man bobsled team in 1932 (above, second from front).

Ágnes Keleti

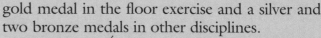

Á gnes Keleti was one of Hungary's gymnastic hopefuls looking forward to the 1940 Olympics, but the Games were cancelled because of World War II. Though this was a serious setback for Ágnes, it could not compare to what would happen to her during the war. In 1940 the Hungarian gymnastic club expelled Ágnes because she was Jewish.

When Nazi Germany moved their forces into Hungary in 1941, the Keleti family went into hiding. Though her sister and mother were saved, her father was sent to Auschwitz, where he died.

Ágnes was able to purchase false identity papers and spent the war working as a maid.

When peace came in 1945, Ágnes still harbored her Olympic dream. She went into serious training when

gold medal in the floor exercise and a silver and two bronze medals in other disciplines.

Amazingly, Ágnes made the Olympic team once again at the age of 35. In Melbourne, Australia, in 1956, she accomplished one of the great unknown feats in Olympic history. She won four gymnastic gold medals—in the floor exercise, balance beam, asymmetrical bars and as part of the Hungarian portable apparatus team, an event that is no longer contested in the Olympics. Ágnes is still in the record book as the oldest gymnast gold medal winner in the Olympics.

After this, Ágnes became a citizen of Israel.

she learned that the Olympic Games would be renewed in London in 1948. At the late age of 27 Ágnes made the Hungarian team.

Three days before the competition was to begin, tragedy again struck Ágnes Keleti. During a training session she tore a ligament in her ankle. She spent the time in London as a spectator on crutches.

But Ágnes wouldn't quit. When the 1952 Olympic Games came to Helsinki, Finland, she was 31. She again made the Hungarian team and then impressed the athletic world by winning a

There she married a Hungarian, who had also left Hungary to become an Israeli citizen. She had two children when she was 42 and 44 years old. Ágnes Keleti's determination and ability to overcome life's setbacks had led her from an incredible athletic career to a rewarding family life. Her reply when people questioned her age at the time of the births: "They didn't believe I could win a gold medal when I was thirty-five and I won four. My children were just two more gold medals."

Daley Thompson   1984 Los Angeles   Great Britain

The scene was Los Angeles, on the afternoon of August 9, 1984. Great Britain's defending Olympic decathlon champion Daley Thompson was in the worst crisis of his career. Jurgen Hingsen, his great rival from West Germany, was dangerously close to catching up to him after six events in the 10-event decathlon. The winner would earn the title of "the world's greatest all-around athlete."

After the first day's events—the 100 meters, long jump, shot put, high jump and 400 meters—Thompson led Hingsen by 114 points. The second day would include the 110-meter hurdles, discus, pole vault and javelin, ending with the grueling 1,500-meter run.

The discus was the seventh event. Hingsen immediately let Thompson know the challenge was on. On his second attempt Hingsen hurled the discus 166 feet, 9 inches, his greatest throw ever and a decathlon Olympic record.

Thompson failed miserably on his first two attempts. His best effort was more than 30 feet shorter than Hingsen's.

With each man having one throw left, an incredible point swing in favor of Hingsen was a distinct possibility. If neither athlete improved on his final attempt, the 6-foot, 7-inch German champion would take the lead.

Thompson began his twirling motion that would generate the power for his throw. "This was my test...this was my moment," Thompson recalled. "Everything that has gone before has no meaning," he'd told himself.

When Thompson's throw landed, the crowd roared. Thompson wiggled his hips like a belly dancer, then jumped in the air. He knew he'd thrown his best distance ever, even though it was 14 feet less than Hingsen's best effort. Thompson still was in first place by 32 points.

Thompson went on to demolish Hingsen in the pole vault and javelin, then leisurely moved through the 1,500 meters, having only to finish the race to ensure his victory.

Daley Thompson had won his second straight decathlon gold medal, defeating Hingsen by 124 points.

Tony Sailer

Austria's Tony Sailer amazed the world by becoming the first man to sweep all three alpine skiing events. At the 1956 Games in Cortina d'Ampezzo, Italy, his opponents couldn't come close to matching his speed.

Sailer's first event was the giant slalom, and when the competition was finished, he'd won the gold by an amazing 6.2 seconds. "I couldn't believe it," said Sailer. "I told them it was impossible, that they should check their watches. I knew that I was skiing fast. But winning by more than six seconds—that is impossible."

Two days later Sailer was in the slalom, which requires making two runs down a twisting course of gates and sharp turns. "I was the fastest in both runs and again my margin of victory was difficult to believe," said Sailer. "I had won by four full seconds!"

Then came the treacherous downhill, on a day plagued by strong winds. The course was so dangerous that more than one-third of the 75 men who entered failed to make it to the finish line.

"A few minutes before I started my run I noticed that one of my ski bindings had broken and I had to borrow a binding from an old friend who was a coach of the Italian team," recalled Sailer. "My coach was very nervous and he kept banging me on the shoulder to make sure I was ready. He kept saying, 'Don't be nervous, you'll make it.' That was very strange because I wasn't at all nervous. He was nervous. And I kept thinking, if he puts his hand on my shoulder one more time I'm going to hit him."

Again in complete control, Sailer's downhill run was as impeccable as his two previous gold medal victories. He won by an overwhelming margin—three and one-half seconds—in one of the greatest individual performances to take place at the Olympics.

John Devitt & Lance Larson

1960 Rome

Australia/United States

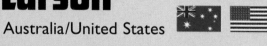

The greatest controversy in the history of Olympic swimming —the duel between John Devitt of Australia and Lance Larson of the United States—took place in the 100-meter freestyle at the 1960 Olympics in Rome, Italy.

With 20 meters left in the race, Devitt was inches ahead of Larson, but the American was gaining with each powerful stroke as they neared the wall for the finish.

As soon as Larson touched the wall underwater, he immediately looked for his time on the scoreboard. Devitt touched above the water, which was easier for the judges to see. This was the era before electronic timing was used to eliminate the possibility of human judging error.

The six judges who were assigned to decide first and second place were evenly divided. Three picked Larson and three picked Devitt.

The chief judge, who traditionally had no vote, illegally broke the tie and ruled that Devitt was the winner.

However, there were three "unofficial" timers assigned to each lane. All three of Devitt's timers clocked him in at 55.2 seconds. The timers in Larson's lane caused an unprecedented dilemma. One timer caught Larson at 55 seconds flat and the other two timed the American at 55.1. All three timers had Larson finishing in a faster time than the Australian.

United States officials protested, but the decision stood. Devitt remained the winner, with Larson the silver medalist.

The final embarrassment came later. Since it's impossible for the second-place finisher to have a time faster than the winner, Larson's time was changed to that of Devitt. Both are now listed in the record book with the identical times of 55.2 seconds.

Wilma Rudolph

1960 Rome   United States 🇺🇸

There is perhaps no Olympic champion who had greater hardships to overcome than Wilma Rudolph. As a child she needed a brace on her left leg to walk after suffering illnesses that included double pneumonia and scarlet fever. Wilma not only shed the brace when she was 11, but went on to win three gold medals at the 1960 Olympics in Rome, Italy.

After years of therapy, Wilma became a basketball star in high school. Her speed on the court

impressed Ed Temple, coach of the famed Tennessee State Tigerbelles track team.

"Coach Temple invited me to attend his summer camp," Wilma remembers. "My dad didn't want me to leave home. I had been so sheltered he was afraid of me going into the outside world."

Her father finally gave in, and the following year, at age 16, Wilma made the Olympic team for the 1956 Games in Melbourne, Australia. She ran the third leg on the 4 x 100-meter relay team that won the bronze medal.

Before the 1960 Rome Olympics, Wilma gave birth to a baby girl. Though she had a child to take care of, it was now predicted that Wilma would become the star of the Games.

A day before she was to compete in her qualifying heat of the 100 meters, the first of her three events, she tripped over a water main and severely sprained her ankle. For a

time it was uncertain whether she'd make it to the starting line. Fortunately the swelling subsided the night before her event, but she had to tape her ankle throughout the competition.

After winning the 100 meters, she won the 200 meters and then ran the anchor leg on the victorious 4 x 100-meter relay team. She now was the darling of the Games and holder of the title of "the fastest woman in the world."

But what really endeared Wilma to millions was her reply to the often asked question, "What was the victory that was most important to you?"

"Oh, without question it was the relay," she always replied. "For then I could stand on the podium with my Tigerbelle teammates whom I love...and we could celebrate together."

Maurilio De Zolt

1994 Lillehammer

Italy

Thousands of Norwegians gathered at the cross-country course at the 1994 Winter Olympics in Lillehammer, Norway, to witness the men's 4 x 10-kilometer relay.

In Albertville two years earlier the Norwegians had won all five men's cross-country events, including the relay. Here in Lillehammer they'd already won the first three men's events, adding up to eight successive victories in two Olympics. Only Italy and Finland were given a chance of upsetting the Norwegians in the relay.

The first leg was perhaps the most critical part of the race, especially for the Italian team. Their chances for winning were dependent on the "old man," 43-year-old Maurilio De Zolt. De Zolt started his Olympic career 14 years earlier at the 1980 Lake Placid Games. He was 29 then, and he won no medals. However, he won silver medals in the grueling 50-kilometer races in Calgary and Albertville when he was 37 and 41 years old.

"People wonder how I lasted so long. Well, I believe in special foods and drink—particularly pasta and a lot of good red wine," De Zolt explained.

When the race got under way, Norway, Finland and Italy left the rest of the field behind.

At the first passoff the crowd was amazed, not that Norway and Finland were inches apart for the lead, but that 43-year-old Maurilio De Zolt was in third place and only 10 seconds behind.

De Zolt's performance gave inspiration to the Italian team. In the final 100 meters of the race Italy's Silvio Fauner, an outstanding sprinter, took the lead. Italy won the gold medal and broke Norway's gold medal streak of eight straight Olympic cross-country victories.

After the victory ceremony Fauner said, "Through the years people have asked me who is my hero, who is my inspiration. The answer is simple, for he is the same person... his name is Maurilio De Zolt."

The Last Man in the Marathon

1968 Mexico City   Tanzania

The marathon is an exciting event in any year, as runners push themselves to extreme levels of endurance to complete the over-26-mile race. But during the 1968 Mexico City Olympics, three runners performed such great feats that the race is considered a truly historic event.

One of the runners, Abebe Bikila from Ethiopia, was famous for having won consecutive Olympic marathons at the Rome and Tokyo Games. He was the only runner who'd ever accomplished this. He hoped to win a third successive race in Mexico City, to make his career even more exceptional.

Bikila was running strong as he began the marathon. But a third of the way into the race he suddenly dropped out. He'd been suffering for several weeks from a hairline fracture in his left leg and could run no more.

Mamo Wolde, another Ethiopian runner, saw Bikila drop out and immediately poured on the speed, as if he were filling his fallen teammate's shoes. Wolde gave Ethiopia its third successive marathon victory, which he later dedicated to Bikila.

But the drama of this marathon did not end when Wolde crossed the finish line. A little more than an hour later word was passed to the press box and filtered to the few thousand remaining spectators in the stands: "Here comes the last runner in the marathon."

Into the stadium came John Stephen Akhwari of Tanzania. His leg was bloody and bandaged. Wincing with pain at every step, he pressed on. The spectators began a slow, steady clapping. As Akhwari made his painful way around the track, the cheering grew louder. The trek around the course seemed endless, but finally Akhwari hobbled across the finish line. The crowd roared as if this last runner had been the winner.

In the press box one columnist wrote, "Today we have seen a young African runner who symbolizes the finest in the human spirit...a performance that gives meaning to the word courage...all honor to John Stephen Akhwari."

Afterward Akhwari was asked why he had endured the pain. Akhwari appeared perplexed. Then he simply said, "I don't think you understand. My country did not send me to Mexico City to start the race. They sent me to finish the race."

Vladimir Salnikov

1988 Seoul

USSR

Sunday evening, September 25, 1988, at the Seoul Olympic natatorium (a building which houses an indoor swimming pool) in South Korea promised to be a memorable event. It was the final Olympic appearance of Vladimir Salnikov of the Soviet Union. Salnikov was a swimming legend: From 1978 to 1986 he was virtually unbeatable at the 400-, 800- and 1,500-meter freestyle distances. But at age 28 he was considered past his prime.

At the 1980 Moscow Games in the USSR, Salnikov had won three gold medals. His 1,500-meter victory created history—he became the first man to swim the distance in under 15 minutes. Breaking this barrier in swimming was equal to Roger Bannister breaking the four-minute mile!

For almost 10 years Salnikov was unbeaten in the 1,500-meters, racking up 61 consecutive victories. But two years before the Seoul Games, he came in fourth in the 1,500-meter World Championships and failed to qualify for the European championship 1,500-meter final.

Totally depressed, Salnikov sought out a new coach, his wife, Marina. "We worked well together," said Salnikov. "My friends told me I should retire but Marina always cheered me up. She would always say, 'You can do it.'"

The final of the 1,500-meter freestyle was the last event on the Seoul Olympic swimming program. Salnikov swam powerfully, but with 100 meters left, he was exhausted.

"I told myself there is no fifteen hundred meters today...all I can go is fourteen hundred meters," remembers Salnikov. "But then, when I touched the wall with one hundred meters left, I said to myself, 'OK...I change my mind. I will go another hundred meters.'"

During the last 50 meters, the crowd was chanting, "Vladimir...Vladimir...." Vladimir was not going to quit! He pushed himself through his exhaustion to victory—and the cheers began reverberating even louder throughout the stadium..."Vladimir...Vladimir!"

After the award ceremony, Salnikov announced his retirement: "When someone reaches the top, one feels that he has done all he set out to do. I can say yes, I did everything, but that does not mean it is over. Now I must find another mountain to climb."

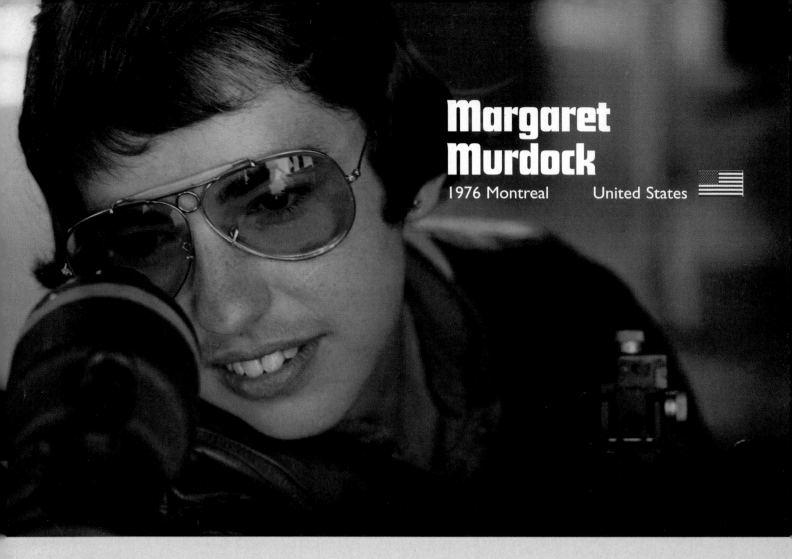

Margaret Murdock

1976 Montreal   United States

Margaret Murdock is considered one of the great Olympic champions in United States history—one of the few women to compete on an equal basis with men at the Olympics. In small-bore rifle competitions, she's won seven individual world championships and 14 world team championships, and holds numerous world records. She is the only woman to ever be ranked in the world's top 10 greatest shooters list by the International Shooting Union.

Murdock also became the first female member of a United States Olympic shooting team. The mother of a small child and in her last year of nursing school, Margaret went to Montreal for the 1976 Games. The competition consists of shooting at targets from three positions: prone, standing and kneeling. The favorite in the event was Lanny Bassham of the United States, who had won the silver medal four years before. When the last rounds were fired, Murdock's name stood

first on the scoreboard with 1,162 points, one more than Bassham.

But as the Americans prepared for the victory ceremony, it was announced that one of the judges had written a 9 on Bassham's score when it should have been a 10. Now Murdock and Bassham were in a tie, each with 1,162 points. Further investigation of the rules determined there were measures to break ties. Bassham's score included three 100s to two for Murdock. Bassham was awarded the gold medal and Murdock the silver.

Bassham took his place on the top step of the victory platform. As "The Star-Spangled Banner" was about to be played, he reached down and clasped Murdock's hand, beckoning her to join him on the top step of the podium. Together they shared the highest step.

"I wanted to show that I felt her performance equaled mine," said Bassham afterward. "There was no way she deserved to stand lower while the anthem was played."

Dan Jansen

1994 Lillehammer   United States

At the 1984 Olympics in Sarajevo, Yugoslavia, 18-year-old Dan Jansen of the United States was happy he'd finished in fourth place in the 500-meter speedskating event. He was only thirty-six-hundredths of a second behind the gold medal winner.

In the next Olympics, held in Calgary, Jansen had to face this challenge knowing that his sister Jane was dying of leukemia. "On the morning of the 500-meter race Mom called and told me that Jane probably wouldn't make it through the day," Jansen recalled. "I talked to Jane one last time and told her I was going to win for her...."

Jansen started off the 500-meter race swiftly. But less than 100 meters later he took a bad fall. Four days later in the 1,000 meters Jansen again fell.

At the 1992 Games in Albertville, France, Jansen finished fourth in the 500 meters and a disastrous 26th in the 1,000 meters. Jansen would make one more try at the 1994 Games. At this point he was the world-record holder in the 500 meters.

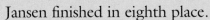

In Lillehammer, Norway, Jansen again started off quickly in the 500 meters. In the stands his wife, Robin, was cheering him on. Robin's mother was holding their nine-month-old daughter, Jane, named after Jansen's sister, who had died six years ago on this day.

"I thought he looked great," remembered Robin. "Then on the last turn I saw the ice fly and I knew he slipped. I turned to my mother and screamed, 'I can't believe this is happening again!'"

Jansen finished in eighth place.

Next was the 1,000-meter race, the last race of his Olympic career. Dan Jansen skated his greatest race ever, breaking the world record by eleven-hundredths of a second.

After the medal ceremony Jansen took a victory lap with his daughter, Jane. The two moved around the track to the thunderous cheers of the thousands of spectators. Dan Jansen had done what he intended to do. As he put it: "I do not try to be better than anybody else. I only try to be better than myself."

Jeff Farrell 1960 Rome

United States

In the spring of 1960 Jeff Farrell of the United States looked forward to the Olympic swimming trials. Farrell held the best time in the world in the 100-meter freestyle that year and was equally superb in the 200-meter freestyle. At the Games in Rome, Italy, he hoped to swim in the 100-meter freestyle and be the anchor man of the 4 x 100-meter medley relay and 4 x 200-meter freestyle relay.

A week before the Olympic trials Farrell woke in the middle of the night with intense stomach pains. He was rushed to the hospital, where it was discovered that his appendix had burst. An emergency operation saved his life.

The Olympic Committee was not going to require Farrell to swim in the trial competitions, but he declined this special consideration. Six days after his operation he appeared at the trials for the 100-meter freestyle. The stitches from his appendectomy had not yet been removed. Despite this major handicap, Farrell amazed his country by winning his place in the final.

The final was extremely close; Farrell finished third. In 1960 only the first two finishers qualified for the 100-meter freestyle. "I lost out by a tenth of a second," Farrell said. "A few meters from the finish I got tangled up in one of the lane ropes and it probably cost me half a second."

A few days later the 200-meter freestyle was scheduled to select the relay team. Again, Farrell made it to the final. "I missed the one-hundred-meter freestyle team by inches," recalled Farrell. "In the two-hundred meters I thought I had a chance to win."

All eyes were on Farrell as the swimmers thrashed through the water. He needed to finish in the top six in order to make the Olympic team. One newspaper columnist wrote afterward, "Never had so many spectators been cheering for a man to finish sixth."

Farrell did better than that. He finished fourth in the 200 meters and now was in a good position to be selected for both relay teams.

The incredible saga of Jeff Farrell reached its climax a few months later at the Rome Olympics. There, a healthy Farrell anchored both United States relay teams to two Olympic gold medals and two world records.

Yasuhiro Yamashita

1984 Los Angeles   Japan

More than 4,000 spectators filled the arena at the Los Angeles Olympics in 1984 to witness the open division judo championship that featured one of the greatest athletes in modern sports—Yasuhiro Yamashita of Japan.

Yamashita is a national hero in his country, where judo was founded over a century ago. Translated, *judo* means "the gentle way." It emphasizes strength, technique and concentration as opposed to violence. Judo players are told that "yielding is strength….Bend like a bamboo, then strike back."

Yamashita had a string of 194 straight wins over a seven-year period. Most of these victories were won by ippons, the equivalent to a knockout in boxing. But Yamashita still had one more goal. "I have wanted to win an Olympic gold medal since I was a child. I missed an opportunity in 1980 when the boycott prevented me from competing in the Moscow Olympics," recalled Yamashita.

He won his first Olympic bout in less than 30 seconds, but in defeating another opponent, Yamashita severely injured a muscle in his right leg. He left the mat limping and in great pain. In judo it is considered acceptable for an opponent to attack an injury. In subsequent rounds Yamashita had to repeatedly ward off attacks to his injury.

Moving into the final, his opponent was Mohammed Rashwan of Egypt, who'd won all three of his previous bouts easily, all by ippons.

"In my semifinal, it was the first time I ever thought I might lose," said Yamashita later. "My injury was very painful and prevented my normal movement. But I had to forget the pain for my last fight."

Yamashita was spectacular, confidently deflecting the powerful blows to his injured leg. After only a few seconds, he threw Rashwan to the mat, then slowly lowered his body onto the Egyptian. The referee raised his hand to signal a victory. Yasuhiro won the gold medal and fulfilled the philosophy of judo: "Yielding is strength….Gentle turns away sturdy."

Joan Benoit 1984 Los Angeles

United States

Joan Benoit, the United States distance runner, won the first women's Olympic marathon gold medal. This medal signified two victories—one for all female athletes, and a more personal one for Joan herself.

Years before Joan's achievement, at the 1928 Olympics in Amsterdam, the Netherlands, several women collapsed at the finish of the 800-meter run and had to be treated for exhaustion. It was decided that, for their own safety, women couldn't compete in distances longer than 200 meters at the Olympics.

It took more than a half century, but women finally got their chance at an Olympic marathon on August 5, 1984. Joan Benoit led the pack at this historical moment at the Los Angeles Coliseum. As she crossed the finish line at the end of the 26-mile, 385-yard run, only a few knew what a superhuman effort Joan had made to reach this point.

Just 11 weeks before the Olympics, the marathon trials were held to select the three women who would represent the United States. Benoit had recovered from double Achilles surgery—a painful operation on the important tendon just above the heel and below the calf of the leg—in the year

before the trials and was now her country's best bet for the marathon. However, less than two months before the trials, Benoit began to have pains in her right knee so severe that her running motion was impaired. She was treated by her doctor, but the pain recurred. Benoit not only couldn't run—she could barely walk.

Normal surgery wouldn't have allowed her to recover in time for the trials. So, just over two weeks before the trials, she decided to undergo arthroscopic surgery, which at that time wasn't the conventional treatment. Five days later there was no pain in her right leg. However, she'd been overcompensating to protect the weakened knee, resulting in a painful hamstring injury to her left leg.

One week before the trials, Benoit was prepared to give up, but she continued to have her legs treated, and on the morning of the trials decided to give it her best. She won the trials only 17 days after her operation!

The climax to the story came on August 5, when Joan took a victory lap around the Los Angeles Coliseum, waving an American flag to an adoring crowd as the winner of the first women's Olympic marathon gold medal.

Murray Rose & Tsuyoshi Yamanaka

1956 Melbourne

Australia/Japan

No one could have predicted that the 1,500-meter freestyle swimming final would be the most memorable event of the 1956 Olympics in Melbourne, Australia. It would be another confrontation between two great young swimmers—Murray Rose of Australia and Tsuyoshi Yamanaka of Japan, both 17 years old. Though they were good friends because of the many times they'd met at the pool, Rose and Yamanaka never showed any evidence of their friendship in public. World War II had been over for only 11 years, and many Australians hadn't yet forgotten the war, when their country was in danger of being invaded by Japan.

In Melbourne Rose defeated Yamanaka in the 400-meter freestyle. Next was the 1,500-meter event. Before the starter gun went off, neither boy would look at the other. The race was a close one, but with each lap Rose moved farther and farther ahead. With 100 meters left, Rose was in front by 6 meters. Yamanaka kept cutting down the distance but it was not enough. Rose won by 2 meters. Rose won a third gold medal as a member of the Australian 4 x 200-meter freestyle relay team. Murray Rose's three victories made him the youngest male triple gold medal winner ever in Olympic swimming.

"We looked at each other for a few seconds," remembered Rose. "For years there was still some resentment in Australia toward the Japanese. I knew the crowd was watching us closely. Then, simultaneously, we both smiled, fell over the lane lines and warmly embraced. Behind us we heard the crowd cheering. But the true significance of our race and what happened afterward was on the front page of every newspaper the next day. One of the captions read, 'The war is finally over.'"

An additional fact about that day made it even more special: The 1,500-meter race took place on December 7, 1956—exactly 15 years to the day after Japan's attack on Pearl Harbor and their subsequent declaration of war against the United States, Australia and their allies.

USA-USSR Basketball

The greatest basketball controversy in the history of the Olympics took place at the 1972 Munich Games during the final between the United States and the Soviet Union.

The United States had won every gold medal in basketball since the sport was added to the Olympic program in 1936. U.S. teams were undefeated in 62 straight games over eight Olympic competitions. The only question left in Munich was how big a margin the United States' victory would be.

But the game didn't go as the Americans expected. When the official clock showed three seconds left in the game, the United States led 50 to 49. The Soviets put the ball in play. The ball got to midcourt when the referee's whistle blew with one second left.

A conference was held at the scorers' table and it was decided that even though the Soviets had called an illegal time-out, they would be given a second opportunity to throw the ball in. The clock was reset to show three seconds left.

The Soviets threw the ball in and took a long, desperate shot from midcourt. It missed. The buzzer sounded and the United States apparently won 50 to 49.

The Soviets again converged on the scorers' table and protested that the clock hadn't been set back to the original three seconds. Many people were astonished when the decision was made to reset to the original three seconds.

The Americans protested to no avail. For the third time the Soviets were able to put the ball in play. This time they made the basket, and the buzzer sounded with the Soviets in front 51 to 50.

The United States protested, petitioning the International Olympic Committee with sworn statements by the referee and timekeeper that the Soviet victory was illegal. But the protest was denied and the Soviet Union was declared the winner of the gold medal.

Perhaps the most vivid image of the great controversy is of a photograph taken at the medal award ceremony. Standing on the top step of the victory podium is the Soviet team, and to their left is the team from Cuba, the bronze medal winner. The silver medal level is empty. The United States team refused to appear, and to this day none of the players on the team have accepted their second-place medals.

Mark Spitz 1972 Munich

United States

Mark Spitz of the United States created Olympic history at the 1972 Games in Munich, Germany, by winning seven gold medals in swimming, all world records. But Spitz almost turned down his chance to go for all seven golds.

In his first event he easily won the 200-meter butterfly. A few hours later Spitz swam the anchor leg in the 4 x 100-meter freestyle relay for his second gold medal. When the individual 100-meter times for the relay swimmers were released, Spitz's teammate and chief rival in the 100 meters, Jerry Heidenreich, was twelve-hundredths of a second faster than Spitz. Some experts predicted that Heidenreich would beat Spitz in the upcoming 100-meter freestyle.

In the next three days Spitz easily won three more gold medals swimming in the 200-meter freestyle, in the 100-meter butterfly and as the anchor leg for the American 4 x 200-relay team. This was a total of five gold medals and five world records.

It was then that an exhausted Spitz had a conversation with his coach, Sherm Chavoor. "I said, 'Coach, I think it would be better if I "scratched" from the one-hundred-meter freestyle and saved myself for the four-by-one-hundred medley relay,'" Spitz recalled. "Six gold medals isn't so bad."

"You mean five gold medals," said Chavoor with sarcasm.

"What do you mean?" said Spitz.

"Listen, Mark, if you don't swim the one hundred meters, you're out of the relay. You might as well go home now," Chavoor said. "They'll say you're 'chicken'—that you're afraid to face Jerry Heidenreich."

Spitz took his coach's advice and beat Heidenreich by a few feet in the 100 meters. He then climaxed a brilliant seven-gold-medal, seven-world-record performance as part of the victorious 4 x 100-meter medley relay team.

Before the podium ceremony, his three teammates lifted Spitz to their shoulders and took a victory lap around the pool. Spitz had this photograph framed.

"That picture with my teammates holding me high above them I enjoy more than the one that was taken with the seven gold medals around my neck," Spitz said. "Having a tribute from your teammates is a feeling that can never be duplicated."

Betty Cuthbert

1956 Melbourne /
1964 Tokyo
Australia

In the history of women's track and field, Australian Betty Cuthbert's amazing achievements are often overlooked. Though the 18-year-old Cuthbert was the star of the Games in Melbourne, Australia, in 1956 there was no worldwide television to publicize this. Her outstanding feats were limited to newspaper reports.

Cuthbert was entered in three events in Melbourne—the 100 meters, 200 meters and 4 x 100-meter relay. In the final of the 100 meters, Cuthbert wasn't the favorite, but she won easily.

"It was very exciting because the hundred meters was not my favorite event," Cuthbert recalls. "I love the two hundred and thought I had a good chance in that one."

Betty was correct. She won the gold in the 200, as well as the adoration of all of Australia.

A few days later Betty anchored the Australian 4 x 100-meter relay team to victory to win her third gold. Could she duplicate this feat four years later at the 1960 Olympics in Rome, Italy?

Sadly, Rome was a nightmare for Betty. An injured hamstring acted up in the second round of the 100 meters and she was eliminated. The injury caused her to withdraw from the 200 meters and the 4 x 100-meter relay.

"I retired in 1960 for the simple reason I thought I had done enough," Cuthbert recalled. "But then this little voice in my head kept waking me up every night and telling me I should run again. So then I made the decision to try again at the 1964 Tokyo Games and immediately I was able to sleep. The voice stopped talking to me."

The event she chose was the 400 meters. For Cuthbert, a sprinter, this was a new event. She had the speed to win, but was uncertain about her ability to last the distance. However, at the Tokyo Olympics Cuthbert crossed the finish line 2 feet in front of the competition. Betty Cuthbert had done what many thought impossible. Eight years after winning three gold medals, she had won a fourth.

Greg Barton

1988 Seoul

One of the favorites in the kayak event at the 1988 Olympic Games in Seoul, South Korea, was 28-year-old Greg Barton of the United States.

Barton's task was a formidable one. Kayaking had been on the Olympic program since the 1936 Games, but no American had ever won a gold medal in the sport.

Greg Barton was a summa cum laude graduate from the University of Michigan and a mechanical engineer. As a child he had daily chores on his parents' farm in Homer, Michigan. It was there he developed the strength he'd need to compete in athletics, for Greg Barton had a physical handicap: He was born with a club foot.

"With all the surgery and physical problems I went through," said Barton, "I think it made me tougher mentally. When the training was getting tough, I would say to myself, 'This is not as tough as what I had to endure to get here.'"

The 1,000-meter race was a close one throughout. Barton stayed near the leaders, then, with 200 meters left, he took the lead. As he approached the finish line, Grant Davies of Australia made his move and both crossed the finish line as one. Neither knew who was the winner.

"The scoreboard flashed that Davies had beaten me by thirty-seven-hundredths of a second," said Barton, "and I was resigned that I had won the silver medal."

But the officials had made a mistake. After a long delay and with meticulous viewing of the electronic finish photograph, the scoreboard flashed the news. Barton won by one-hundredth of a second.

Barton didn't have time to celebrate, since he and Norm Bellingham were scheduled to race next in the 1,000-meter doubles. Their finish in the doubles was almost as close as Barton's victory in the singles. The Americans won by twenty-nine-hundredths of a second.

By a combined total margin of thirty-hundredths of a second, Greg Barton made Olympic history—the first American to win a kayak gold medal and the first kayaker ever to win two gold medals in 90 minutes.

Eleanor Holm

1932 Los Angeles/1936 Berlin   United States

America's Eleanor Holm has a unique Olympic story. She is perhaps more famous for not competing than for winning her gold medals.

As "the baby" of the 1928 Olympic swim team in Amsterdam, the Netherlands, 15-year-old Eleanor Holm finished fifth in the 100-meter backstroke. Four years later at the 1932 Los Angeles Games Eleanor won the 100-meter backstroke.

After the Games she married the popular band leader Art Jarrett and became a singer with his band. In the evenings she would appear with her husband for their nightclub dates and by day she would train at pools in whatever city she was in.

She was a favorite to win the gold medal at the 1936 Games in Berlin, Germany. Aboard the ship that was taking the team to Berlin, Eleanor was seen drinking both wine and champagne. After she paid no heed to the reprimands of the United States Olympic Committee, she was removed from the team. Eleanor tried to convince USOC president Avery Brundage that she was, in fact, adhering to the regulations team members were expected to follow.

"The regulations stated," said Eleanor, "that all team members should continue the same training preparations that we were accustomed to having in the States. That's all I was doing. At home it was my custom to have a glass of wine or champagne every day after a workout."

Despite petitions from many of her fellow athletes for her reinstatement, she was barred from the competition. Even though she had disobeyed regulations, they thought the punishment of not allowing her to compete was too severe.

"I'm still very bitter about what Avery Brundage did," says Eleanor sadly. "He not only lost a certain gold medal for me, but a gold medal for the United States. But I got even with him. The Germans couldn't understand how they would do such a thing so I was invited to all the Embassy parties as their guest. And whenever Mr. Brundage showed up he would stay a few minutes, then leave with the maddest look on his face. He didn't like the fact that all the photographers were taking pictures of me and not him."

John Ian Wing

1956 Melbourne　　　　　　　　　　Australia

John Ian Wing, a 17-year-old Australian of Chinese parentage, was an Olympic champion at the 1956 Games in Melbourne, Australia. He didn't win a gold medal, nor did he compete in any athletic event. All John Ian Wing did was write a simple, poignant letter to the Melbourne Olympic Organizing Committee.

There was much strife in the world at this time. The Hungarian revolt became bloody when the Soviet Union sent troops and tanks into Budapest, even as the Hungarian team was making its way to Melbourne. Nevertheless, the Games continued and were a success.

A few days after the opening ceremonies Sir Wilfred Kent Hughes, the head of the Melbourne Olympic Organizing Committee, received John's letter.

"Dear Friends," the letter began.

"I am a Chinese boy and have just turned seventeen years of age. Before the Games I thought everything would be in a muddle. However, I am quite wrong. It is the most successful Games ever staged…. Mr. Hughes, I believe it has been suggested a march be put on during the closing ceremonies and you said it couldn't be done. I think it can be done…. The march I have in mind is different than the one during the Opening Ceremony…. During the march there will be only one nation…what more could anybody want if the whole world could be made as one nation?"

Thus began a tradition that would remain for all the Olympic Games to come. Men and women athletes from many nations would say a final farewell as one nation, as opposed to marching under their own national flag.

Unfortunately John Ian Wing was not among the many thousands who witnessed the final procession in Melbourne. A chorus of hundreds sang words that were specially written for the ceremony: "Momok Wonargo Ora Go-Yai." These Aboriginal words meant, "Farewell, brother, by and by come back."

John Ian Wing's letter had changed the closing ceremonies forever.

Lawrence Lemieux

1988 Seoul   Canada 🍁

The sailing competition was under way at Pusan, not far from South Korea's capital of Seoul, the main site for the 1988 Olympics. Sailing alone near the halfway point on the Finn-class racecourse was Lawrence Lemieux of Edmonton, Canada. Lemieux was then in second place in the race, the fifth of a seven-race event. He had a good chance of winning one of the medals.

The conditions for sailing had become unexpectedly dangerous. Acceptable winds of 15 knots per hour had escalated at times to 35 knots. Nearby, in the 470 class, two sailors on the Singapore team, Joseph Chan and Shaw Her Siew, were thrown into the water, suffering injuries and unable to right their boat. The situation was a dangerous one.

Lemieux immediately took action, forgetting his own race and sailing toward Joseph Chan. As the Canadian was dragging Chan aboard, even his own boat began filling with water. After rescuing Chan, Lemieux immediately headed toward Shaw Her Siew, who was clinging to his overturned boat. Lemieux rescued the second man, and now both sailors were in his boat. But for Lemieux victory was impossible. He waited for an official patrol boat to reach him, then transferred the two men to safety.

Lemieux continued in his race, but the loss of time during the rescue operation put him out of contention. He finished 22nd in a race that started with 32 boats.

Soon after the race, the story of the rescue reached the jury of the International Yacht Racing Union. They unanimously decided that Lemieux should be awarded second place for this race—the position he was in when he went to the aid of the Singapore crew. None of the other contestants questioned the decision.

Though Lemieux didn't win a medal in the overall seven-race competition, at the medal award ceremony President Juan Antonio Samaranch, President of the International Olympic Committee, paid honor to Lemieux for his act.

"By your sportsmanship, self-sacrifice and courage," said Samaranch, "you embody all that is right with the Olympic ideal."

Mike Boit

1976 Montreal

Kenya

Mike Boit, Kenya's great middle-distance runner, was one of the favorites to win the 800 meters at the 1976 Games in Montreal. Four years earlier in Munich, Germany, Mike had won the bronze medal in this event, just one-tenth of a second behind the winner.

The day before the race Mike heard the news: Kenya had joined the African boycott of the Montreal Games. The African countries wanted the International Olympic Committee to bar New Zealand from competing in Montreal. The New Zealand rugby team months earlier had accepted an invitation to play in South Africa—a country that had been barred from competing in the Olympics because of their policies of racial discrimination. When the petition was turned down, African countries decided to leave en masse before the Games got under way. Only Senegal and Ivory Coast decided to stay.

Boit had been looking forward to one of the great 800-meter finals in Olympic history, when he would face Alberto Juantorena of Cuba and Rick Wohlhuter of the United States.

But unfortunately Mike stayed on at Montreal as only a spectator. He watched intently as the runners went off in the 800-meter final. As Juantorena finally took over the lead, Mike leaned forward as if he were moving with the great Cuban champion.

When Juantorena crossed the finish line an easy winner, Mike's eyes followed him as the Cuban waved to a cheering crowd. Juantorena had set a world record, and in doing so became the first gold medalist from a non-English-speaking country in the 800 meters.

Mike was silent as Juantorena continued around the track in a victory lap. When asked if he thought he could have won the race, Mike paused, and then tears started down his face. "We'll never know, will we?" he said. "We'll never know."

Eamonn Coghlan

1988 Seoul

Ireland

If an athlete were ever to be considered the perfect symbol of the Olympic philosophy "to enter the arena…make the attempt and pursue excellence," then runner Eamonn Coghlan of Ireland would be the unanimous choice.

At the 1976 Games in Montreal, with one lap to go, 23-year-old Eamonn Coghlan was in the lead of the 1,500-meter race. But Coghlan was passed by three runners and finished fourth.

In the 1980 Moscow Games in the USSR, Coghlan would try the 5,000 meters. A few weeks before the Moscow Games Coghlan was hit by a stomach flu and his training was intermittent. In the end he again had to settle for fourth place.

In the following years misfortune plagued him. He lost a year of training and competition due to injury, and within a short period of time the three most influential men in his life died—his father, his high school coach and Jumbo Elliott, his coach at Villanova University.

Early in 1983 he set the world indoor mile record (which still stands today), but his major sights were focused on winning a world championship. He entered the 5,000-meter race to be held at the 1983 World Championships in Helsinki, Finland.

Coghlan fulfilled his dream. He won the 5,000-meter World Championship and became one of the favorites to win a medal at the 1984 Los Angeles Olympics. But again tragedy struck. A stress fracture in his shin bone returned and he couldn't compete at the 1984 Olympics.

In 1988, at the age of 35, Coghlan faced the starter's pistol for the 5,000-meter semifinal race in the Seoul Games in South Korea. Coghlan was among the leaders during the early part of the race, but with each lap he fell farther behind. He finished 28th out of 30 starters and didn't qualify for the final.

After the race, Coghlan, in the tradition of the great Irish poets, said, "I can hold my head up high, I think, for the rest of my life and say, I really tried…but it wasn't to be. I went to the Olympic Games because that's what it's all about. Making the effort…being a sportsman…being a true sportsman."

Bonnie Blair

1988 Calgary/1992 Albertville/1994 Lillehammer

 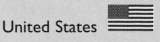

Bonnie Blair was 19 when she competed in the Olympics for the first time at the 1984 Games in Sarajevo, Yugoslavia. With her mother and two sisters watching, she finished eighth in the 500 meters. This was the beginning of what the speed-skating world would come to call "the Blair Bunch," the group of family and friends that would follow Bonnie to cheer her on in her magnificent career.

At the 1988 Games in Calgary, about 30 of the Blair Bunch showed up to watch Bonnie. She broke the world record in the 500 meters by two-hundredths of a second and won her first gold medal.

Four years later in Albertville, France, about 45 of the Blair Bunch came to watch Blair win two more gold medals in the 500 and 1,000 meters.

"You know, a lot of people think that I'm under a lot of pressure with my family and friends spending all that money to follow me around," said Bonnie. "But, you know, they don't care whether I win or lose. They'd come anyway 'cause we're one big family that's having lots of fun…"

More than 60 of the Blair Bunch came to see Bonnie skate in Lillehammer, Norway, in 1994. If she won the 500 meters, she'd become the first speed skater, male or female, to win three successive gold medals in the same event.

Bonnie's skating was spectacular. At intermission, when the ice was to be resurfaced, Bonnie broke precedent. With the event still on, she decided to celebrate. "I wanted to hug my mom and the rest of my family and friends," she said, laughing. "It didn't matter that the competition wasn't over. I just wanted to be with them."

She again made Olympic history with her third successive 500-meter gold medal. A few days later she won the 1,000 meters for the second time…the last race of her Olympic career.

As Bonnie took her final victory lap around the track, one columnist was writing the lead to his story: "Throughout history many Olympic heroes have been created. Bonnie Blair invented herself."

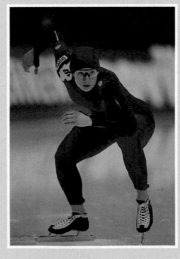

Emil Zátopek

1948 London/1952 Helsinki   Czechoslovakia

Emil Zátopek of Czechoslovakia will never forget what happened at the 1952 Olympics in Helsinki, Finland. The great Czech distance runner had just won the 5,000 meters, his third Olympic gold medal. A few days before, he had won the 10,000-meter race, adding to the gold and silver he had earned running in the London Olympics four years earlier.

Now in Helsinki, as he left the ceremony for the 5,000-meter winners, Zátopek noticed that the women competing in the javelin event were entering the field. One of those women was his wife, Dana. He rushed over to her and proudly showed her his latest gold medal. "Emil, let me have it. I will hold it for good luck," Dana said. Emil handed it to her.

On her first throw of the javelin, Dana broke the Olympic record, and no one could match her outstanding performance. The Zátopeks became the only married couple to ever win Olympic gold medals on the same day at the Summer Games. Dana happily savored their victory during the remaining days in Helsinki, but Emil became bored.

Then he made an announcement that came as a great surprise to everyone: "I think I'll try the marathon."

To the amazement of his fans and fellow athletes, Emil lined up for the 26-mile, 385-yard event, a race he'd never run before.

"I was told that Jim Peters of Great Britain was the heavy favorite to win the marathon," said Zátopek. "So before the race, I asked if he would mind if I ran with him." A surprised Peters agreed.

"The pace in the beginning was very fast," Emil said. "I was so tired and Jim was running like he could do this forever. So I said to him, 'Isn't the pace too fast?'"

Jim replied in jest, "No, it's too slow."

But Emil thought Jim Peters was serious. "So rather than wait for Jim, I ran faster and left him behind," Emil explained. "I just kept on running and when I entered the stadium, the 80,000 people were screaming, 'Zátopek... Zátopek...Zátopek,' and I won my third gold medal in Helsinki. After I crossed the finish line, they told me that Jim Peters collapsed from exhaustion along the route and they had to take him to the hospital."

Medal of Eternal Friendship

1936 Berlin

It was just past nine in the evening on August 5, 1936, and only a few lights illuminated the pole vault area at the Olympic Stadium in Berlin, Germany. The competition had continued longer than expected. Unlike today, the Berlin stadium had no high-intensity lighting that could turn night into day. A few thousand spectators sat in near darkness to witness the climax of a very close competition.

The three finalists battling for the pole vault medals were Earl Meadows of the United States and two close friends from Japan, Shuhei Nishida and Sueo Oe. For Nishida, this would be his second successive chance to win the gold medal. At the 1932 Los Angeles Games he had to settle for the silver.

The bar stood at the Olympic record of 14 feet 3¼ inches. On his second try Meadows cleared. Nishida and Oe missed all three attempts. As the crowd cheered Meadows, Nishida and Oe congratulated him. The two Japanese then continued to jump for second and third place, but darkness ended the competition before a final outcome could be determined.

"Oe and I went back to the Olympic Village certain we had tied, since we both jumped identical heights," Nishida remembered. But overnight officials made a surprising decision, one that was never fully explained.

"I awoke the next morning to find out that I was awarded the silver medal and my teammate Oe the bronze," Nishida said. "But I was not happy with the decision. When we got back to Japan both Oe and I agreed that we would have our silver and bronze medals cut in half. Then we joined half of the silver medal with half of the bronze medal, which we would both keep. This made us very famous, for the medals were called the Medals of Eternal Friendship.

"Sadly these are the remaining memories I have of my friend and teammate Sueo Oe, because he was killed in the Philippine campaign at the start of World War II. But his memory lives on for all of Japan. His medal remains on display at the National Stadium in Tokyo."

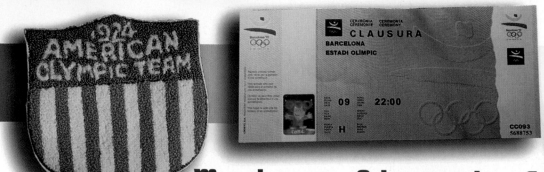

Modern Olympic Sites

	Year	Site	Nations	Total	Men	Women
1st Olympiad	1896	Athens, Greece	14	ca 245	ca 245	0
2nd Olympiad	1900	Paris, France	26	1,225	1,206	19
3rd Olympiad	1904	St. Louis, Missouri	13	687	681	6
Intercalated Games	1906*	Athens, Greece	20	884	877	7
4th Olympiad	1908	London, England	22	2,035	1,999	36
5th Olympiad	1912	Stockholm, Sweden	28	2,547	2,490	57
6th Olympiad	1916	*Canceled due to WWI*				
7th Olympiad	1920	Antwerp, Belgium	29	2,668	2,591	77
8th Olympiad	1924	Paris, France	44	3,092	2,956	136
9th Olympiad	1928	Amsterdam, Netherlands	46	3,014	2,724	290
10th Olympiad	1932	Los Angeles, California	37	1,408	1,281	127
11th Olympiad	1936	Berlin, Germany	49	4,066	3,738	328
12th Olympiad	1940	*Canceled due to WWII*				
13th Olympiad	1944	*Canceled due to WWII*				
14th Olympiad	1948	London, England	59	4,099	3,714	385
15th Olympiad	1952	Helsinki, Finland	69	4,925	4,407	518
16th Olympiad	1956	Melbourne, Australia	72	3,342	2,958	384
17th Olympiad	1960	Rome, Italy	83	5,346	4,738	610
18th Olympiad	1964	Tokyo, Japan	93	5,140	4,457	683
19th Olympiad	1968	Mexico City, Mexico	112	5,530	4,750	781
20th Olympiad	1972	Munich, Federal Republic of Germany	121	7,123	6,065	1,058
21st Olympiad	1976	Montreal, Canada	92	6,028	4,781	1,247
22nd Olympiad	1980	Moscow, USSR	80	5,217	4,092	1,125
23rd Olympiad	1984	Los Angeles, California	140	6,797	5,230	1,567
24th Olympiad	1988	Seoul, Republic of Korea	159	8,465	6,279	2,186
25th Olympiad	1992	Barcelona, Spain	169	9,367	6,659	2,708
26th Olympiad	1996	Atlanta, Georgia	(est) 197	10,000		
27th Olympiad	2000	Sydney, Australia				

Olympic Winter Games

	Year	Site	Nations	Total	Men	Women
Winter Events**	1908	London, England	5	21	14	7
Winter Events**	1920	Antwerp, Belgium	10	86	74	12
1st Winter Games	1924	Chamonix, France	16	258	245	13
2nd Winter Games	1928	St. Moritz, Switzerland	25	464	438	26
3rd Winter Games	1932	Lake Placid, New York	17	252	231	21
4th Winter Games	1936	Garmisch-Partenkirchen, Germany	28	668	588	80
5th Winter Games	1948	St. Moritz, Switzerland	28	669	592	77
6th Winter Games	1952	Oslo, Norway	30	694	585	109
7th Winter Games	1956	Cortina d'Ampezzo, Italy	32	820	688	132
8th Winter Games	1960	Squaw Valley, California	30	665	522	143
9th Winter Games	1964	Innsbruck, Austria	36	1,091	891	200
10th Winter Games	1968	Grenoble, France	37	1,158	947	211
11th Winter Games	1972	Sapporo, Japan	35	1,006	800	206
12th Winter Games	1976	Innsbruck, Austria	37	1,123	892	231
13th Winter Games	1980	Lake Placid, New York	37	1,072	839	233
14th Winter Games	1984	Sarajevo, Yugoslavia	49	1,274	1,000	274
15th Winter Games	1988	Calgary, Canada	57	1,423	1,110	313
16th Winter Games	1992	Albertville, France	64	1,801	1,313	488
17th Winter Games	1994	Lillehammer, Norway	67	1,844	1,302	542
18th Winter Games	1998	Nagano, Japan				
19th Winter Games	2002	Salt Lake City				

*While historians do not usually consider them to be a true Olympic Games, most acknowledge that the Intercalated Games injected new spirit into the Olympics, such as the addition of a first true Opening Ceremonies. Athletes, such as Ray Ewry later in this list, are often credited with medals won there. His lifetime total is ten medals, including the two he won in 1906; not including them, his lifetime total is eight.
**Although figure skating was an event at both the 1908 and 1920 Games, and an ice hockey tournament was contested in 1920, an authorized, official Olympic Winter Games did not emerge until 1924.

Olympic Facts

Excerpted from *The Golden Book of the Olympic Games* by Bill Mallon and Erich Kamper • Milan, Italy • Villardi & Associati, 1993

Olympic Records

Most Medals
18 Larisa Latynina (URS-GYM)
15 Nikolay Andrianov (URS-GYM)
13 Edoardo Mangiarotti (ITA- FEN)
13 Takashi Ono (JPN-GYM)
13 Boris Shakhlin (URS-GYM)
12 Sawao Kato (JPN-GYM)
12 Paavo Nurmi (FIN-ATH)
11 Matthew Biondi (USA-SWI)
11 Vera Cáslavská (TCH-GYM)
11 Viktor Chukarin (URS-GYM)
11 Carl Osburn (USA-SHO)
11 Mark Spitz (USA-SWI)

Most Gold Medals
10/8 Ray Ewry (USA-ATH)*
10 Ray Ewry (USA-ATH)
9 Larisa Latynina (URS-GYM)
9 Paavo Nurmi (FIN-ATH)
9 Mark Spitz (USA-SWI)
8 Matthew Biondi (USA-SWI)
8 Sawao Kato (JPN-GYM)
8 Carl Lewis (USA-ATH)
7 Nikolay Andrianov (URS-GYM)
7 Vera Cáslavská (TCH-GYM)
7 Viktor Chukarin (URS-GYM)
7 Aladár Gerevich (HUN-FEN)
7 Boris Shakhlin (URS-GYM)

Most Silver Medals
6 Shirley Babashoff (USA-SWI)
6 Aleksandr Dityatin (URS-GYM)
6 Mikhail Voronin (URS-GYM)
5 Eleven athletes tied with five each

Most Bronze Medals
6 Heikki Savolainen (FIN-GYM)
5 Philip Edwards (CAN-ATH)
5 Adrianus de Jong (NED-FEN)
5 Daniel Revenu (FRA-FEN)
5 Harri Kirvesniemi (PIN-NSK)

Most Years Between Appearances
40 Ivan Osiier (DEN-FEN, 1908-48)
40 Magnus Konow (NOR-YAC, 1908-48)
40 Paul Elvstrom (DEN-YAC, 1948-88)
40 Durward Knowles (GBR/BAH-YAC, 1948-88)
36 Francois La Fortune Sr. (BEL-SHO, 1924-60)
36 Kroum Lekarski (BUL-EQU, 1924-60)
36 Nelson Pessoa Filho (BRA-EQU, 1956-92)

Most Medals, Women
18 Larisa Latynina (URS-GYM)
11 Vera Cáslavská (TCH-GYM)
10 Polina Astakhova (URS-GYM)
10 Àgnes Keleti (HUN-GYM)
10 Raisa Smetanina (URS/EUN-NSK)
9 Nadia Comaneci (ROM-GYM)
9 Lyudmila Turishcheva (URS-GYM)
9 Lyubov Yegorova (EUN/RUS-NSK)
8 Seven athletes tied with eight each

Most Gold Medals, Women
9 Larisa Latynina (URS-GYM)
7 Vera Cáslavská (TCH-GYM)
6 Kristin Otto (GDR-SWI)
6 Lidiya Skoblikova (URS-SSK)
5 Polina Astakhova (URS-GYM)
5 Àgnes Keleti (HUN-GYM)
5 Bonnie Blair (USA-SSK)
5 Nadia Comaneci (ROM-GYM)
5 Nelli Kim (URS-GYM)

Most Silver Medals, Women
6 Shirley Babashoff (USA-SWI)
5 Larisa Latynina (URS-GYM)
5 Mariya Gorokhovskaya (URS-GYM)
5 Raisa Smetanina (URS/EUN-NSK)
5 Andrea Ehrig-Schone-Mitscherlich (GDR-SSK)
4 Six athletes tied with four each

Most Bronze Medals, Women
4 Marja-Liisa Kirvesniemi-Hamalainen (FIN-NSK)
4 Margit Korondi (HUN-GYM)
4 Larisa Latynina (URS-GYM)
4 Sofiya Muratova (URS-GYM)
4 Merlene Otty [-Page] (JAM-ATH)
4 Yelena Valbe (EUN-NSK)

Most Years Winning Medals, Women
5 Ildikó Ságiné-Ujlakiné-Rejto (HUN-FEN)
5 Raisa Smetanina (URS/EUN-NSK)
4 Yelena Belova-Novikova (URS-FEN)
4 Galina Gorokhova (URS-FEN)
4 Galina Kulakova (URS-NSK)

119

4 Inna Ryskal (URS-VOL)
4 Tatyana Samusenko-Petrenko (URS-FEN)
4 Irena Szweinska-Kirszenstein (POL-ATH)

Most Years Winning Gold Medals, Women
3 Thirteen athletes tied with three each

Most Years Between Medals, Women
16 Ilona Elek (HUN-FEN)
16 Liselott Linsenhoff (FRG-EQU)
16 Ellen Muller-Preis (AUT-FEN)
16 Ildikó Ságiné-Ujlakiné-Rejto (HUN-FEN)
16 Raisa Smetanina (URS/EUN-NSK)
16 Olga Szabo-Orban (ROM-FEN)

Most Years Between Gold Medals, Women
16 Raisa Smetanina (URS/EUN-NSK)
12 Seven athletes tied with twelve each

Most Appearances, Women
7 Kerstin Palm (SWE-FEN, 1964-88)
6 Janice Lee York-Romary (USA-FEN, 1964-92)
6 Lia Manoliu (ROM-ATH, 1952-72)
6 Christilot Hansen-Boylen (CAN-EQU, 1964-76, 1984, 1992)
6 Marja-Liisa Kirvesniemi-Hamalainen (FIN-NSK 1976-94)
5 Twelve athletes tied with five each

Most Years Between Appearances, Women
28 Jessica Newberry-Ranschousen (USA-EQU, 1960-88)
28 Christilot Hansen-Boylen (CAN-EQU, 1964-92)
24 Ellen Muller-Preis (AUT-FEN, 1932-56)
20 Seven athletes tied with 20 each

Most Medals, Men
15 Nikolay Andrianov (URS-GYM)
13 Edoardo Mangiarotti (ITA-FEN)
13 Takashi Ono (JPN-GYM)
13 Boris Shakhlin (URS-GYM)
12 Sawao Kato (JPN-GYM)
12 Paavo Nurmi (FIN-ATH)

Most Gold Medals, Men
10/8 Ray Ewry (USA-ATH)*
9 Paavo Nurmi (FIN-ATH)
9 Mark Spitz (USA-SWI)
8 Matthew Biondi (USA-SWI)
8 Sawao Kato (JPN-GYM)
8 Carl Lewis (USA-ATH)

Most Silver Medals, Men
6 Mikhail Voonin (URS-GYM)
6 Aleksander Dityatin (URS-GYM)
5 Seven athletes tied with five each

Most Bronze Medals, Men
6 Heikki Savolainen (FIN-GYM)
5 Philip Edwards (CAN-ATH)
5 Adrianus de Jong (NED-FEN)
5 Daniel Revenu (FRA-FEN)
4 Nine athletes tied with four each

Most Years Winning Medals, Men
6 Aladár Gerevich (HUN-FEN)
6 Hans Gunter Winkler (FRG-EQU)
5 Ten athletes tied with five each

Most Years Between Medals, Men
28 Aladár Gerevich (HUN-FEN)
28 Alfréd Hajós (HUN-SWI/ART)
28 Tore Holm (SWE-YAC)
24 Eight athletes tied with 24 each

Most Years Between Gold Medals, Men
28 Aladár Gerevich (HUN-FEN)
24 Reiner Klimke (FRG/GER-EQU)
24 Pál Kovács (HUN-FEN)
24 Edoardo Mangiarotti (ITA-FEN)
20 Manlio Di Rosa (ITA-FEN)
20 Lars Jorgen Madsen (DEN-SHO)
20 Hubert Van Innis (BEL-ARC)

Most Appearances, Men

8 Paul Elvstrom (DEN-YAC,
      1948-60, 1968-72, 1984-88)
8 Raimondo d'Inzco (ITA-EQU,
      1948-76)
8 Durward Knowles (GBR/BAH-YAC,
      1948-72, 1988)
8 Hubert Raudaschi (AUT-YAC,
      1964-92)
8 Piero d'Inzco (ITA-EQU, 1948-76)
7 Four athletes tied with seven each

Most Years Between Appearances, Men

40 Ivan Osiier (DEN-FEN, 1908-1948)
40 Magnus Konow (NOR-YAC,
       1908-48)
40 Paul Elvstórm (DEN-YAC, 1948-88)
40 Durward Knowles (GBR/BAH-YAC,
       1948-88)
36 Francois La Fortune, Sr. (BEL-SHO,
       1924-60)
36 Kroum Lekarski (BUL-EQU,
       1924-1960)
36 Nelson Pessoa Filho (BRA-EQU,
       1956-92)

Youngest Medalist, Overall

(age in years and days)
<10   Unknown French boy* in 1900
          (ROW)
10-218 Dimitrios Loundreas
          (GRE-GYM, 1896)
11-302 Luigina Giavotti (ITA-GYM,
          1928)
12-024 Inge Sorensen (DEN-SWI, 1936)
12-218 Ines Vercesi (ITA- GYM, 1928)
12-233 Noel Vandernotte (FRA-ROW,
          1936)
12-271 Clara Marangoni (ITA-GYM,
          1928)
13-024 Dorothy Poynton (USA-DIV,
          1928)
13-268 Marjorie Gestring (USA-DIV,
          1936)
13-283 Klaus Zerta (FRG-ROW, 1960)
13-283 Kim Yoon-Mi (KOR-STK, 1994)

Youngest Known Competitors, Overall

<10   Unknown French boy* in 1900
          (ROW)
10-218 Dimitrios Loundreas
          (GRE-GYM, 1896)
11-078 Cecilia Colledge (GBR-FSK, 1932)

11-108 Megan Taylor
          (GBR-FSK, 1932)
11-162 Beatrice Hustiu
          (ROM-FSK, 1968)

*The Dutch coxed pairs (rowing) qualified with a heavy coxswain, and then picked a small boy from the shore to sit in the cox's seat for the final. The team won.

Oldest Medalist, Overall

72-279 Oscar Swahn (SWE-SHO, 1920)
68-193 Samuel Duvall (USA-ARC, 1904)
66-155 Louis Noverraz (SUI-YAC, 1968)
64-257 Oscar Swahn (SWE-SHO, 1912)
64-001 Galen Spencer (USA-ARC, 1904)
63-239 Robert Williams (USA-ARC,
          1904)
61-244 John Butt (GBR-SHO, 1912)
61-131 Bill Roycroft (AUS-EQU, 1976)
60-264 Oscar Swahn (SWE-SHO, 1908)
60-103 William Milne (GBR-SHO,
          1912)

Oldest Known Competitors, Overall

72-280 Oscar Swahn (SWE-SHO, 1920)
72-048 Arthur von Pongracz
          (AUT-EQU, 1936)
70-330 Durward Knowles (BAH-YAC,
          1988)
70-005 Lorna Johnstone (GBR-EQU,
          1972)
68-229 Roberto Soundy (ESA-SHO,
          1968)

Official Country Abbreviations

AFG	Afghanistan	DEN	Denmark	LAT	Latvia	SIN	Singapore
AHO	Neth. Antilles	DJI	Djibouti	LBA	Libya	SLE	Sierra Leone
ALB	Albania	DOM	Dominican Republic	LBR	Liberia	SLO	Slovenia
ALG	Algeria	ECU	Ecuador	LES	Lesotho	SMR	San Marino
AND	Andorra	EGY	Egypt	LIB	Lebanon	SMY	Smyrna
ANG	Angola	ESA	El Salvador	LIE	Liechtenstein	SOL	Solomon Islands
ANL	Antilles (W. Indies)	ESP	Spain	LTU	Lithuania	SOM	Somalia
ANT	Antigua	EST	Estonia	LUX	Luxembourg	SRI	Sri Lanka
ARG	Argentina	EUN	Unified Team (CIS)	MAD	Madagascar	SUD	The Sudan
ARM	Armenia	FIJ	Fiji	MAR	Morocco	SUI	Switzerland
ARU	Aruba	FIN	Finland	MAL	Malaysia	SUR	Suriname
ASA	American Samoa	FRA	France	MAW	Malawi	SVK	Slovakia
AUS	Australia	FRG	Federal Rep. of Germany	MCD	Macedonia	SWE	Sweden
AUT	Austria	GAB	Gabon	MDV	Maldives	SWZ	Swaziland
AZE	Azerbaijan	GAM	The Gambia	MEX	Mexico	SYR	Syria
BAH	The Bahamas	GBR	Great Britain	MGL	Mongolia	TAN	Tanzania
BAN	Bangladesh	GDR	German Demo. Rep.	MLD	Moldova	TCH	Czechoslovakia
BAR	Barbados	GEO	Georgia	MLI	Mali	TGA	Tonga
BEL	Belgium	GEQ	Equatorial Guinea	MLT	Malta	THA	Thailand
BEN	Benin	GER	Germany	MON	Monaco	TJK	Tadzhikistan
BER	Bermuda	GHA	Ghana	MOZ	Mozambique	TKM	Turkmenistan
BHU	Bhutan	GRE	Greece	MRI	Mauritius	TOG	Togo
BIR	Burma	GRN	Grenada	MTN	Mauritania	TPE	Chinese Taipei
BIZ	Belize	GUA	Guatemala	MYA	Myanmar	TRI	Trinidad & Tobago
BLS	Belarus	GUI	Guinea	NAM	Namibia	TSL	Thessalonika
BOH	Bohemia	GUM	Guam	NCA	Nicaragua	TUN	Tunisia
BOL	Bolivia	GUY	Guyana	NED	The Netherlands	TUR	Turkey
BOT	Botswana	HAI	Haiti	NEP	Nepal	UAE	United Arab Emirates
BRA	Brazil	HKG	Hong Kong	NGR	Nigeria	UES	USSR/Estonia
BRN	Bahrain	HON	Honduras	NIG	Niger	UGA	Uganda
BRU	Brunei	HUN	Hungary	NOR	Norway	UKR	The Ukraine
BSH	Bosnia-Herzegovina	INA	Indonesia	NZL	New Zealand	ULA	USSR/Latvia
BUL	Bulgaria	IND	India	OMA	Oman	ULI	USSR/Lithuania
BUR	Burkina-Faso	IOP	Independent Olympic Participant	PAK	Pakistan	URS	Soviet Union
CAM	Kampuchea			PAN	Panama	URU	Uruguay
CAN	Canada	IRI	Iran	PAR	Paraguay	USA	United States
CAY	Cayman Islands	IRL	Ireland	PER	Peru	UZB	Uzbekistan
CEY	Ceylon	IRQ	Iraq	PHI	The Philippines	VAN	Vanuatu
CGO	Congo	ISL	Iceland	PNG	Papua New Guinea	VEN	Venezuela
CHA	Chad	ISR	Israel	POL	Poland	VIE	Vietnam
CHI	Chile	ISV	U.S. Virgin Islands	POR	Portugal	VIN	St. Vincent & the Grenadines
CHN	China	ITA	Italy	PRK	DPR Korea (North)		
CIS	Commonwealth of Independent States	IVB	British Virgin Islands	PUR	Puerto Rico	VOL	Upper Volta
		JAM	Jamaica	QAT	Qatar	YAR	Yemen AR (North)
CIV	Ivory Coast	JOR	Jordan	RHO	Rhodesia	YEM	Yemen
CMR	Cameroon	JPN	Japan	ROM	Romania	YMD	Yemen DR (South)
COK	Cook Islands	KEN	Kenya	RUS	Russia	YUG	Yugoslavia
COL	Colombia	KGZ	Kergizstan	RWA	Rwanda	ZAI	Zaire
CRC	Costa Rica	KOR	Korea (South)	SAF	South Africa	ZAM	Zambia
CRO	Croatia	KSA	Saudi Arabia	SAM	Western Samoa	ZIM	Zimbabwe
CUB	Cuba	KUW	Kuwait	SCO	Scotland		
CYP	Cyprus	KZK	Kazakhstan	SEN	Senegal		
CZE	Czech Republic	LAO	Laos	SEY	Seychelles		

Three-Letter Sport Abbreviations

ARC	Archery	FTB	Football Association (Soccer)	RUG	Rugby Football
ASK	Alpine Skiing	GYM	Gymnastics	SHO	Shooting
ATH	Athletic (Track & Field)	HAN	Team Handball	SKE	Skeleton
BAS	Basketball	HOK	Hockey (Field)	SSK	Speed Skating
BIA	Biathlon	ICH	Ice Hockey	SWI	Swimming
BOB	Bobsledding	JUD	Judo	TEN	Tennis (Lawn Tennis)
BOX	Boxing	LAX	Lacrosse	TOW	Tug-of-War
CAN	Canoe & Kayaking	LUG	Luge	TTN	Table Tennis
CYC	Cycling	MOP	Modern Pentathlon	VOL	Volleyball
DIV	Diving	MTB	Motorboating	WAP	Water Polo
EQU	Equestrian Events	NSK	Nordic Skiing	WLT	Weightlifting
FEN	Fencing	POL	Polo	WRE	Wrestling
FSK	Figure Skating	ROW	Rowing and Sculling	YAC	Yachting

Olympic Ceremonies and Traditions

Olympic Flag

The Olympic flag has a plain white background with no border. In the center are five interconnected rings. They form two rows of three rings above and two below. The rings of the upper row are, from left to right, blue, black and red. The rings of the lower row are yellow and green.

The rings are thought to symbolize the five continents, Europe, Asia, Africa, Australia and America. The colors of the rings are thought to have been chosen because at least one of these colors can be found in the flag of every nation. It is not certain that this was the intent of the flag's designer.

The flag was presented by Baron Pierre de Coubertin in 1914 at the Olympic Congress in 1914, celebrating the 20th anniversary of the founding of the International Olympic Committee. It was flown that year at Alexandria, Greece, but made its Olympic début in 1920 at Antwerp. The "primary" Olympic flag was thus known as "the Antwerp flag." In 1984, Seoul presented a new Olympic flag (as the old was getting quite worn) to the IOC, which was first flown at the 1988 Olympics.

At the closing ceremonies of the Olympic Games, the mayor of the Olympic host city presents the Olympic flag to the mayor of the next Olympic host city. The flag is then kept in the town hall of the host city until the next Olympic Games.

Olympic Motto

"Citius, altius, fortius" — a Latin phrase meaning "swifter, higher, stronger." De Coubertin adopted it after hearing of its use by Father Henri Martin Didon of Paris. Didon, later headmaster of Arcueil College, used the phrase while describing the athletic accomplishments of his students at that school. He had previously been at the Albert Le Grand school, where the Latin words were carved in stone above the main entrance.

Olympic Creed

"The most important thing in the Olympic Games is not to win but to take part, just as the most important thing in life is not the triumph, but the struggle. The essential thing is not to have conquered but to have fought well."

This is the current form of the creed as it appears on the scoreboard at the Opening Ceremonies of the Olympic Games, although many permutations of this basic message have been seen.

De Coubertin adopted, and later quoted, this creed after hearing Ethelbert Talbot, the Bishop of Central Pennsylvania, speak at St. Paul's Cathedral on July 19, 1908, during the London Olympics. The service was given for the Olympic athletes, who were all invited.

Talbot was in London for the 5th Conference of Anglican Bishops (usually called the Lambeth Conference). During the conference, many of the visiting bishops spoke in various churches. Talbot's exact words that day were:

"The important thing in these Olympics is not so much winning as taking part."

Olympic Oath

"In the name of all competitors, I promise that we shall take part in these Olympic Games, respecting and abiding by the rules which govern them, in the true spirit of sportsmanship, for the glory of sport and the honor of our teams."

Written by de Coubertin, the oath is taken by an athlete from the host country, while holding a corner of the Olympic flag. It is also given by a judge from the host country, with slightly different wording. The athlete's oath was first given in 1920 in Antwerp by Belgian fencer Victor Boin.

The original wording ended with "countries," but it was changed in the 1960s because of the IOC's desire to eliminate nationalism at the Olympics.

Olympic Flame

The Olympic flame is a symbol reminiscent of the ancient Olympics, in which a sacred flame burned at the altar of Zeus throughout the Olympics. The flame was first used at the modern Olympics in Amsterdam in 1928, and again was lit throughout the 1932 Los Angeles Olympics.

In 1936, Carl Diem, chairman of the organizing committee for the Berlin Olympics, proposed the idea of lighting the flame in ancient Greece and transporting it to Berlin via torch relay. This was done and has been repeated at every Olympic Winter Games since 1952.

The flame is lit in the altis of the ancient Olympic stadium at ancient Olympia, on the Greek Peloponnesus. The flame is lit during a ceremony by women dressed in robes similar to those worn by the ancient Greeks. The flame is lit naturally by the rays of the sun at Olympia and reflected off a curved mirror. A symbolic high priestess then presents the torch to the first relay runner.

This work could not have been completed without the help of three expert collections: ALLSPORT (U.S.A. & U.K.), the United States Olympic Committee and the Amateur Athletic Foundation of Los Angeles. Individual credits, as required, follow:

ALLSPORT 1, 4-5, 16-17, 18, 20, 25, 30 (R), 32 (R), 34, 35, 39, 47, 49, 52, 55 (L), 63, 64, 74, 82, 83 (T), 88, 103 (B), 116
ALLSPORT/ALLSPORT/IOC 40, 46, 66, 108
ALLSPORT/HULTON DEUTSCH 23, 25, 63, 88, 85 (L), 96, 116 (R)
ALLSPORT/USOC 91
STEVE POWELL/ALLSPORT 19, 38 (R), 61, 73, 93
SIMON BRUTY/ALLSPORT 24, 28, 90 (R)
SHAUN BOTTERILL/ALLSPORT 28, 115 (R)
CHRIS COLE/ALLSPORT 28 (B), 101
MIKE POWELL/ALLSPORT 31 (R), 42, 50 (B), 56, 73 (L), 99 (B), 101 (R), 115
TONY DUFFY/ALLSPORT 36, 45, 50 (L), 52, 55, 59, 60, 86, 99, 104, 107, 109, 113, 114
G. ASCHENDORF/ALLSPORT 36 (R)
DAVID CANNON/ALLSPORT 38, 42 (R), 58
VANDYSTADT/ALLSPORT 49 (L), 68 (M), 79
PASCAL RONDEAU/ALLSPORT 50, 90, 97
BOB MARTIN/ALLSPORT 68
GRAY MORTIMORE/ALLSPORT 77
DOUG PENSINGER/ALLSPORT 85 (R)
JOHN GICHIGI/ALLSPORT 103 (T)
JONATHAN DANIEL/ALLSPORT 115 (L)
UNITED STATES OLYMPIC COMMITTEE 30, 40 (R), 44, 46, 50, 53 (L), 63, 66 (R), 75, 82, 106, 110
AMATEUR ATHLETIC FOUNDATION OF LOS ANGELES 2-3, 43 (B), 118-123
THE BETTMAN ARCHIVE 43
UPI/BETTMAN 54, 67, 100 (B)
ASUCLA 72, 80
© IOC, PHOTO BY J.J. STRAHM 8
FRODE NIELSEN 12
© 1988 LONG PHOTOGRAPHY 31 (L)
CAPPY PRODUCTIONS, INC. 82, 99
U.S. BOBSLED & SKELETON FEDERATION 87
TANGMERE MILITARY AVIATION MUSEUM 87 (L)
U.S. ARMY PHOTO 100
CANADIAN SPORT IMAGES 112
PHOTO KISHIMOTO CORPORATION 117 (T)